W9-AAV-060

WHAT PEOPLE ARE SAYING ABOUT
THE POWER OF HOME . . .

"I've personally heard Ted teach on the home for over ten years now. He enjoys his family more than anything else he does in life. *The Power of Home* is a fresh look on what it means to pursue faith and family with passion."

DR. GARY SMALLEY
author of The Key to Your Child's Heart

"Filled with wisdom and insight, Ted Cunningham challenges us to grow our marriages into the great source of joy God intended. Packed with practical tips and personal stories, you'll be inspired and encouraged throughout these pages."

MARGARET FEINBERG
author of Fight Back With Joy

"I absolutely love Ted's heart for marriage and family, and his focus on hope! He is so well-respected in leadership circles as one of the main marriage voices today, and it's easy to see why: his stuff is *so good!* Every page of this book is filled with encouraging perspective, insight, and advice for singles, spouses, and families who want to live out God's callings on their lives and experience the blessings that come as a result!"

SHAUNTI FELDHAHN
social researcher and bestselling author of For Women Only

"Many are struggling to find a way forward on a number of significant issues in our culture. If more would take up the cause of helping families thrive at home the way Ted Cunningham has in *The Power of Home*, the way forward on many of those issues would take care of itself."

JOEL THOMAS

lead pastor of Mission Community Church; previously served sixteen years on staff at North Point Community Church

"As I read *The Power of Home*, I found myself wishing this kind of wisdom had been available to me when I was raising my kids. The best compliment I can give this book is that I plan to give a copy to my kids as a roadmap for raising their children. I love that *The Power of Home* is written by a man who is down in the trenches of everyday family life. Ted Cunningham confronts head-on the cultural trends of family life and shows us a better way . . . God's way. This book is chock-full of practical insight and wisdom. *The Power of Home* will give you a roadmap for making family life not just tolerable, but actually enjoyable."

LANCE WITT

founder of Replenish

"Ted brings forward another fresh cultivation of humor, humility, and biblical wisdom within *The Power of Home*. The transparency and ease with which Ted communicates make him one of the top communicators and authors within the intersections of marriage and family. *The Power of Home* is an easy approach to positively influence the life God calls us to in each of our homes."

MATT ENGEL

Director of Marriage Ministry, Mission Community Church, Gilbert, AZ

"*The Power of Home* is an excellent reminder to husbands and wives to allow *your* marriage to leverage *your* home. A great marriage is a great gift for your children. Invest back into your most important relationships #yourhome."

TIM POPADIC
national director of Date Night Works

"I love the way Ted thinks. He's an imperfect, honest man who takes his role as Christ-follower, husband, and dad super seriously, but he doesn't take himself too seriously. This translates to him taking vital issues and communicating truth in a way that's entertaining and life-changing."

ART VANZANTEN
family ministries pastor, First Assembly of God, Fort Myers, FL

"In Ted Cunningham's new book, *The Power of Home: Taking Charge of Your Faith and Your Family,* he does that thing he does . . . once again! He takes us on a fun and inspiring ride that combines amazing vision with remarkable practicality. He is able to do this for many reasons, but the number one reason is the fact he lives it out with his wife and kids. Read it. Give it to people you love. I promise you will be glad you did!"

TED LOWE
director of MarriedPeople™

"Transparent and helpful—two words that not only describe his latest book *The Power of Home,* but words that truly embody the heart of my friend and pastor, Ted Cunningham. The power behind the words in this book are not only found in their practical application for us as readers, but are also found in the lived-out day-to-day family life of Ted himself. This is a book you can trust to unite your marriage and family closer together from a man who practices what he preaches."

JOSHUA STRAUB, PHD
author of SafeHouse

"There's no greater platform for discipleship than within the walls of our own homes. This book will encourage you to equip your children to impact the world, rather than the world negatively impacting them. Read this book and realize how tangible it is to empower your children! Ted hit a home-run with *The Power of Home*. In order for us to impact our culture we must begin with impacting our own homes!"

ADAM DONYES
founder of the Kanakuk Link Year

"There's so much competing against the home these days: work, culture, technology, sports, busyness, and so much more. In *The Power of Home,* Ted brings us back to the foundational truths about the home and faith. Ted loves Jesus, his family and his church, and out of this love he practically shepherds the reader by providing a road map to help establish the home as the place where we find life in Christ."

SCOTT KEDERSHA
director of premarital ministry, (Merge)Watermark Community Church, Dallas, TX

"Ted is one of today's most gifted communicators as he seamlessly weaves stories and principles in a memorable way. His wisdom with the twenty foxes that spoil the marriage vine and his practical insight on what brings families back to church are contained in two invaluable chapters."

RON HUNTER JR.

executive director and CEO of Randall House, D6 Conference Director and co-author of Toy Box Leadership

"In *The Power of Home* Ted inspires singles, couples, and parents with a healthy view of marriage and family to take ownership of not just their homes, but their own lives as well. Ted teaches you how to define your faith and how to see it lived out in the world. The engaging use of humor and storytelling will equip you and encourage you to face the challenges of life, to enjoy your life and each family relationship. I highly recommend you read *The Power of Home* today and enjoy the blessings of a fulfilling home life!"

DR. ALEX HIMAYA

lead pastor, theChurch.at, Broken Arrow, OK

THE POWER OF HOME

TAKING CHARGE OF YOUR FAITH AND YOUR FAMILY

TED CUNNINGHAM

Copyright © 2015 by Ted Cunninngham
ALL RIGHTS RESERVED
Published by Salubris Resources
1445 N. Boonville Ave.
Springfield, Missouri 65802

No portion of this book may be reproduced, stored in a retrieval system,
or transmitted in any form or by any means—electronic, mechanical,
photocopy, recording, or any other—except for brief quotations in printed
reviews, without the prior written permission of the publisher.

Cover design by PlainJoe Studios (www.plainjoestudios.com)

Interior formatting by Prodigy Pixel (www.prodigypixel.com)

Unless otherwise specified, Scripture quotations used in this book are taken
from the 2011 edition of the Holy Bible, New International Version®. NIV®.
Copyright © 1973, 1978, 1984, 2011 by Biblica, Inc. ™ Used by permission of
Zondervan. All rights reserved worldwide.www.zondervan.com. The "NIV"
and "New International Version" are trademarks registered in the United
States Patent and Trademark Office by Biblica, Inc.™

Scripture taken from *The Message*. Copyright © 1993, 1994, 1995, 1996, 2000,
2001, 2002. Used by permission of NavPress Publishing Group.

ISBN: 978-1-68067-033-2
18 17 16 15 • 1 2 3 4
Printed in the United States of America

To Woodland Hills Family Church,
thank you for inspiring families in the Ozarks
and around the world.

CONTENTS

CHAPTER 1

GUARDING HOME

SIX MARRIAGE AND FAMILY
TRENDS WE MUST CONFRONT

*"Commitment is making the choice
to give up all other choices."*

—SCOTT STANLEY

F aith and family are all that matter. To know God and each other is the most important pursuit in life. My relationship to God and family determines everything about my home. God designed the family to bear His image to the world. What does the world know about God by watching your family?

I married Amy Freitag on October 19, 1996, in Fremont, Nebraska. We had our daughter, Corynn, on August 4, 2003, and our son, Carson, on June 2, 2005. Amy is the Queen. Corynn is the Princess. Carson is the mighty warrior. When people ask me, "What's your role in the family?" I always say, "Lowly servant." Jesus is our King.

We pray together. We enjoy gathering around the table for meals. We play games. We read and memorize Scripture. We disagree. We seek forgiveness. We serve at church. We visit grandparents. We celebrate holidays. We attend weddings and funerals. We rest in the family room almost every night. We are together a lot. Enjoying life and each other is never questioned in our home. We are family.

I'm grateful for the work and ministry of Dennis Rainey and FamilyLife. Their bold commitment to the home challenges me to pursue family above all earthly pursuits. In the FamilyLife Manifesto they clearly define home as the place where we establish life in Christ:

We believe God is the originator of the family. It was established by God in His inaugural act of the marriage between a man and a woman. The Bible further defines the family through God's instruction for married couples to have children, whether by birth or by adoption. We believe the purpose of the family is to glorify and honor God by forming the spiritual, emotional, physical, and economic foundation for individuals, the church, and any society.

It is at home that children see manhood and womanhood modeled. It is at home that moral values are taught by parents and placed into the hearts of their children. It is at home that people see the reality of a relationship with Jesus Christ modeled. It is at home that people learn to live out their convictions. Therefore, we are committed to upholding the concept of family as

God's original and primary means of producing a godly offspring and passing on godly values from generation to generation.[1]

Our faith is defined in the home, then displayed to the world. If you want to know the character of a man, woman, or child, watch them in the home. Taking charge of your faith and family begins with an honest assessment of where you are right now. We won't spend time in this book looking at your past, although you may find yourself going back there from time to time. If you catch yourself reading something and saying, "I wish I could go back and do things differently," pause and pray. We can't go back, but we can be redeemed. There are no perfect families, but every family can be redeemed.[2] The goal of this book is redemption, not regret or judgment.

> *Taking charge of your faith and family begins with an honest assessment of where you are right now.*

WHERE ARE YOU NOW?

Imagine standing in front of the directory map at the mall. I usually start by looking for the "X" next to the words "You Are Here." Then I find the store I want to go to and chart my course. I hate being lost and I love plans.

My parents taught me how to navigate with a gigantic Rand-McNally map. Remember those? I think that atlas was taller than I was when I first started reading it. Both of my parents are excellent with directions. We started our trips on the Illinois page and worked state by state until we arrived at our destination. Boy, how times have changed.

Mobile devices and Google maps changed everything. Now, you simply enter your destination and hit "Route." You don't even need to type in your current location because your phone knows where you are. Once you hit "Route," Maps gives you two to three options you can take with the quickest route highlighted for you. I love choices, so I usually tap on the other routes. Speed limits, distance, and traffic estimate the time. Delays for traffic, weather, accidents, or lawbreakers (and you know who you are) are some of the other variables to consider.

This approach has so intrigued me I now use it in counseling sessions. I like to give people "routes" out of the circumstances. This idea first came to me after a friend of mine went to a week-long counseling intensive with his wife. Within minutes of the first session, they were told, "There are two ways to approach the healing your marriage needs. The first option will take five years and you will each gain about thirty-five pounds. The other option will get to the source of your problem by the end of today." While I can't share with you the details of my friends' counseling, I can tell you that the second option required immediate truth telling and complete personal responsibility. The first option would include more of what got them into the mess to start with: hiding, lying, and fatigue.

Whether it's a mall directory, Rand-McNally, Google Maps, or a counseling session, we all must take a hard look at where we are, where we want to go, and how we're going to get there. Here are three questions to ask yourself as you work through this book:

We are here: What is the current state of my faith and family?

Where we want to go: There are no perfect families, but what does it mean for me and my family to be redeemed?

How will we get there?: How will I take charge of my faith and family?

WE ARE HERE

What the home believes about life, family, and faith is caught in a cultural drift. I don't mean to go all gloom and doom on you, but we do need to get honest about what's happening in the world and church today. As you read through the next few pages, ask the Holy Spirit to call you by name. When you find yourself getting judgmental toward those around you, pause and look in the mirror

> *"You are here" doesn't mean "You must stay here."*

for just a second. If your soul feels regret, take it to the Lord in prayer. Taking charge of your marriage, family, and faith starts with an honest assessment of where you are right now. It may be painful, but the fruit of this labor is so worth it. "You are here" doesn't mean "You must stay here."

These six marriage and family trends threaten the very existence of our churches, communities, and homes:

1. The Kid-Centered Home.

Sometime around 1980, parents became more nurturing than past generations. Opportunity and advantage became the foundation and priority for parenting. We want our children to have every opportunity and shot at success. I like how my friend, Pastor Carey Nieuwhof asked his congregation the question, "When does giving our child every advantage become a disadvantage?" Great question. People who are kid-centered answer that question through many new parenting motives. They become . . .

- Vanity parents who use their children's attributes and accomplishments to impress others

- Perfection parents who set high expectations for success in every opportunity and endeavor

- Competitive parents who compare their children's strengths and weaknesses to other children

- Gifted parents who picture their children as "extra special" so they seek out "extra special" opportunities

- Rescue parents who hover and helicopter over their children, shielding them from all pain, loss, and trials

- Companion parents who seek friendship by elevating a child to the level of spouse or descend as a parent to the level of a sibling.[3]

Kid-centered parents tend to be guilt-prone.

We somehow feel that if we deny our children opportunities or advantages we will damage them. So we give them every shot on the field, on the stage, and in the classroom. We want them to excel and be great at everything they try. We feel defective as a parent if they fail in an attempt. We struggle to prioritize character over competency. As Francis Chan is known for saying, "Our greatest fear should not be of failure but of succeeding at things in life that don't really matter." Are we spending too much time seeking success for our children in the wrong things?

Kid-centered parents are permissive.

Some parents set no rules or guidelines in the home as a reaction to their parents' dominant style. Others set boundaries but are lax in enforcing them. Again, the motives for permissiveness range from fear of hurting the child emotionally to the desire to be best friends with the child.

Kid-centered parents lack rhythm and margin.

The kid-centered home runs at break-neck speed with no room to breathe. We are late to one event or activity because we are coming from another. Kids and parents are tired. Both cry out for a break, but no one knows how to get one. Years ago at a family camp, a lady said to me, "Ted, I feel like all of us are on the crazy bus headed off the cliff and no one is jumping up and down screaming for it to stop before we all die." I think it's time to start jumping up and down and screaming.

Kid-centered parents misunderstand the parent-child bond.

According to Genesis 2:24, the bond between a husband and a wife is to be stronger than the bond between a parent and a child: "That is why a man leaves his father and mother and is united to his wife, and they become one flesh." If you ask my son Carson, "What's your dad's definition of maturity according to Genesis 2:24?" He would say, "I won't be with Mom and Dad forever, so plan accordingly." That's right. I love joking with my kids by saying, "I want you kids to know that your mom and I have big plans after you leave home."

They usually respond with, "What are you going to do?"

"First, we're going to Disney World," I proclaim.

"Dad!!!!" is their confused and frustrated response every time.

2. Prolonged Adolescence.

This second trend is the primary result of the kid-centered home. Biblically and historically, there are two seasons to life: childhood and adulthood. Boys became men and girls became women. In 1904, the term *adolescence* created a gap between childhood and adulthood. This gap continues to grow. My friend, Ryan Pannell, defines prolonged adolescence as "too much privilege and not enough responsibility." It's an extended vacation from the responsibility required to successfully work a job and build healthy relationships.

Parents today accelerate childhood milestones and delay adulthood milestones. For the first ten years of a child's life all they hear is, "Go, go, go!" We've replaced reading in elementary school with accelerated reading. For years now we've watched the My Baby Can Read commercials on television. We start our child's professional sports career around age six or seven.

Parents today accelerate childhood milestones and delay adulthood milestones.

Then around ages ten to twelve (the tween years), two engines kick in. We call these engines individualization and separation. Our children begin pushing back from mom and dad to become little adults. This is when we start to freak out, throw on the brakes, and delay adulthood milestones.

Imagine trying to ride a horse while nudging it in the sides to go and simultaneously pulling back on the reigns. After a few hours, the horse would be exhausted. The same confusion exists in the home today. Mom and dad tell their kids to run and also to slow down in the same breath. This exhaustion in the home leads to the fear of making decisions later in life. The primary example of this is the third trend.

3. Delayed Marriage.

Prolonged adolescence delays adulthood milestones. It keeps young adults from accepting personal responsibility for life, work, and relationships. There are five adulthood milestones that every generation experiences: (1) Leave home; (2) finish school or training; (3) secure employment; (4) get married; and (5) start a family. Until recently, every generation completed those milestones in a very short time. I know some seniors at our church who completed those five milestones in less than a week. True. On the other hand, many young people have not yet reached even one milestone. There are many reasons embraced by young people for this delay.

The independence delay says, "I need to learn how to live on my own before I'll be successful in marriage." To protect their future, young people today hold off marriage. They're told, "You need to learn how to be independent before you can be successful at marriage." *Independence* is the new socially acceptable term for "selfishness." We raise our children in the kid-centered home only to send them off and say, "Go live by yourself and for yourself for another ten years or more." However, couples struggle in marriage when husband and wife want to live independently. Oneness in marriage is tough when spouses want their own way, their own money, and their own lives.

The spreadsheet delay says, "I can't afford to be married." That's a hard statement to hear from someone holding a specialty drink from Starbucks in one hand and the latest iPhone in the other. You can marry early if you don't try to accumulate in three years what your parents accumulated in thirty.

The job delay says, "I must secure the perfect job before settling down." This is probably the second most common delay I hear in our church. When I hear this, I encourage the young person to work any job or multiple jobs until the perfect job comes along. Success in the marketplace largely depends on the combination of your character (hard work) and competency (skills). Work hard as you develop your skills.

A recent article by Robert J. Samuelson in the *Washington Post,* gives updated research on the decline of marriage in our culture:

Even those who know marriage is on the skids— presumably, most of us—may be surprised by the extent of its decline. A little history helps. To Americans coming of age in the 1950s, the expectation was that most would marry. It was part of society's belief structure. And most did. Now these powerful social pressures have faded and, for many, disappeared.

Consider. In 1960, only 12 percent of adults ages 25 to 34 had never married; by the time they were 45 to 54, the never-married share had dropped to 5 percent. Now fast forward. In 2010, 47 percent of Americans 25 to 34 had never married. Based on present trends, this will still be 25 percent in 2030 when they're 45 to 54.[4]

While this trend won't change anytime soon, parents, pastors and professors can begin to paint a beautiful picture of marriage on a regular basis to help young people prioritize matrimony over career, status, money, and independence.

4. Sliding vs. Deciding.

Dr. Scott Stanley from the University of Denver coined this term and it is the name of his blog (www.slidingvsdeciding.com). Couples today are sliding past the decisions of traditional relationship formation. Cohabitation is the primary example of this trend. To protect themselves, there is no definition assigned to the relationship. "Let's just see how this works out" is the socially acceptable explanation for "Let's not commit to anything long-term." Dr. Stanley defines "commitment" as making a choice to give up all other choices. Church leaders and parents teach children to hold off decisions rather than how to make good decisions that lead to and form healthy relationships.

> *Couples today are sliding past the decisions of traditional relationship formation.*

In 1995, I met Amy on a blind date. I decided that night that she was *the one*. I told my buddy that I was going to marry her. The decision was made. Then I had to make another decision to ask her out on a second date.

We dated for several months before I asked her dad for permission to marry her. In May of 1996, in Fremont, Nebraska, I walked into the kitchen where Amy's 6-foot-2-inch, full-blooded Norwegian dad stood. He's a Viking, and I was nervous.

"Mr. Freitag, may I marry your daughter?" I asked.

To which he answered, "You betcha."

I also decided early in this process that I wanted to pay for Amy's final year of college. His answer to that was "You betcha!"

I officially asked Amy that night. She knew it was coming and said, "Yes," over an Italian dinner.

Relationship formation has changed. You go to dinner and think the person across the table is attractive. You date a few times, share a few meals, and then sleep together. After sleeping together a few times, it doesn't make any sense to go home afterwards so you stay all night. A few times spending the night, it doesn't make sense to get up, go home, and get ready for work. So you ask for a drawer or space in the closet. Eventually, you give up one of the two apartments or homes and move in together. You sign a new lease together. Years later, with a couple of pets, you find that you actually made no solid decision but slid into your current arrangement. That is cohabitation.

5. Dating While Divorcing.

Facebook regularly updates us on this trend. A couple you love separates. Weeks after the separation, their profile picture displays a new boyfriend or girlfriend (before divorce papers are drafted). It's difficult to fight for or reconcile in marriage when you have given your heart to another. On top of that, the dating couple want the support of family and friends. That's painful and difficult. We can't, nor should we, celebrate a new relationship while we mourn the death of a marriage. I will not hit the "Like" button on the new profile picture or relationship status update.

A few months back, someone came up to me after a church service where I was guest preaching. He introduced me to his girlfriend. They were living together. He said, "We had an affair. I'm with her now and I love her. I left my wife and kids." I'm listening to the whole story and she isn't saying anything; she's emotional. He's saying he doesn't know what to do. It was obvious that the Holy Spirit gripped both of them. They needed someone to validate the right thing to do.

I asked him, "Is your wife with someone new or remarried?"

He said, "No."

"I know exactly what you should do then. I don't have to pray about it, I don't have to think about it. You need to leave this woman and be reconciled to your wife and family," I said.

They already knew this was the right thing to do. They just needed a loving nudge in that direction. Advocating for children begins with advocating for their parents' marriage.

If you're divorced and remarried, please don't go on a guilt trip with this book. Assess where you are, understand that there are no perfect families, and chart your course towards a healthy, God-honoring marriage and home.

6. Greying Divorce.

Oh, how I wish grandma and grandpa's marriage were safe, but it's not. *The New York Times* brought greying divorce to our attention in 2013:

> "So much for "till death do us part." For the first time, more Americans 50 and older are divorced than widowed, and the numbers are growing as baby boomers live longer. Sociologists call them gray divorcees.

A half-century ago, only 2.8 percent of Americans older than 50 were divorced. While divorce rates over all have stabilized and even inched downward, the divorce rate among people 50 and older has doubled since 1990, according to an analysis of census data by professors at Bowling Green State University in Bowling Green, Ohio. That's especially significant because half the married population is older than 50.

In 1990, 1 in 10 persons who divorced was 50 or older. By 2011, according to the census's American Community Survey, more than 28 percent (more than 1 in 4) who said they divorced in the previous 12 months were 50 or older."[5]

Early one morning when my son was eight years old, we listened to one of my favorite pastors from California, Greg Laurie. He preached from a series called "Happily Even After." The message fit perfectly with what we believe about commitment in marriage and leaving a legacy and inheritance to your children. I leaned over to Carson and said, "Carson, I just want you to know something. I plan to leave you a little something when I die. I just want you to know I'm giving all of it to your mom. More than money, I'm leaving you the legacy of a mom and dad who loved each other and enjoyed life together. You'll appreciate that way more than money."

Robertson McQuilken is the best example of this. After a long and distinguished career at Columbia Bible College, he delivered an emotional resignation letter. At the core of his resignation was his commitment to the "till death do us part" part of the vows:

I haven't in my life experienced easy decision-making on major decisions, but one of the simplest and clearest I've had to make is this one. Because circumstances dictated it. Muriel now, in the last couple of months, seems to be almost happy when with me and almost never happy when not with me. In fact, she seems to feel trapped, becomes very fearful, sometimes almost terrorized, and when she can't get to me there can be anger . . . she's in distress.

But when I'm with her she's happy and contented, and so I must be with her at all times . . . and you can see, it's not only that I promised "in sickness and in health, 'till death do us part,' and I'm a man of my word. But as I have said, . . . it's the only fair thing. She sacrificed for me for forty years, to make my life possible. . . . So if I cared for her for forty years, I'd still be in debt.

However, there's much more. . . . It's not that I have to. It's that I *get to*. I love her very dearly, and you can tell it's not easy to talk about. She's a delight. And it's a great honor to care for such a wonderful person.[6]

Muriel lost her ability to communicate in 1995 and went to be with the Lord in 2003. For the last eight years of her life, Robertson faithfully served her with no ability to communicate with her. He is an inspiration to us all.

WHERE WE WANT TO GO

Each one of these trends is rooted in excessive emotional reliance on others. Codependency plugs into people, places, and things as the source of life. When we misplace the source of life, happiness becomes our chief purpose. We want our children to make us happy, so we hold onto them for longer than necessary. We plug into jobs and money as the source of life, and unnecessarily avoid marriage for fear of losing happiness in the early years of adulthood. When our spouse no longer makes us happy, we look for someone else to make it happen.

We hear it all the time in conditional statements starting with "If":

"If my husband shared his feelings with me, our marriage could be saved."

"If my wife enjoyed sex, our marriage could be saved."

"If my parents had been there for me, I wouldn't be in the mess I'm in right now."

"If my boss lightened up, I would stay with this company."

"If my church offered a singles group, then maybe I could find someone to marry."

"If my town had more singles, I'd find someone good."

"If Washington DC could just get along, our country would recover."

"If we put prayer back in school, it would be easier for my kids to share their faith."

"If my 401K survives the next crash, I should be okay for retirement."

"If my house had more equity, I could afford to take that dream vacation."

Each one of these conditional statements lacks power. Each statement is waiting on someone else to change and take charge.

Why wait on someone else to change when you have the power to change right now? It starts with you, not what's going on around you. Personal responsibility doesn't look to others as the source of life. It refuses to blame or point the finger at people, places, and things.

Bill Rogers is an elder at Woodland Hills Family Church and a retired pastor with over forty years of ministry experience. A few years ago he gave me a plaque that once sat in his office. It simply reads, "Those Who Are Absent Are Protected Here." In other words, we will not talk about the absent spouse. We will talk about you. We won't talk about everything the absent party is doing wrong in the relationship. We are going to talk about you taking charge of your life. When Bill gave me the plaque, he laughed and said, "This is the most important message in a pastor's office." I agree.

For the spouse who says, "I'm not the one with the issues," I say, "Give us a few minutes of digging and we'll find plenty to talk about with you."

Taking charge of your home means, "I'm not going to talk about what's going on around me, but I will focus on the only one I can change . . . *me.*"

Why wait on someone else to change when you have the power to change right now?

The primary passage in the Scripture for personal responsibility and taking charge of your life is Galatians 6:2–5:

Carry each other's burdens, and in this way you will fulfill the law of Christ. If anyone thinks they are something when they are not, they deceive themselves.

Each one should test their own actions. Then they can take pride in themselves alone, without comparing themselves to someone else, for each one should carry their own load.

Christ comes alongside each of us and carries our burdens. His yoke is easy and His burden is light (Matthew 11:30). He is our source of life. We go to Him because we can't do it on our own. Ultimately, He carried our sin burden.

When we come alongside another person and get up under a burden that's too much for them to carry, we imitate Christ. There are some burdens that are too much for one person to carry. This is why we have family. We care for one another. If I don't take charge of my faith and care for my family, I'm worse than an unbeliever (1 Timothy 5:8).

Like me, you may be in a season of life where you carry responsibility for your children and your parents. I come alongside them physically, relationally, emotionally, spiritually, mentally, and financially. Galatians 6:5 says, "for each one should carry their own load." Taking charge of my faith and family means I'm considerate and don't overload other members of the family either relationally, emotionally, or financially. Are you being considerate of your family members and carrying your own load? Do you have members of your family who would rather you carry the whole burden so they can kick back free of responsibility? A family will not thrive if one able member chooses to shirk responsibility and avoid contributing to the needs of other members.

Owning your personal spiritual journey and carrying the burdens of others is part of the overflow of Jesus being your Source of Life. Jesus explains this in Matthew 22:37–39:

Jesus replied: "'Love the Lord your God with all your heart and with all your soul and with all your mind. This is the first and greatest commandment.' And the second is like it: 'Love your neighbor as yourself.'"

When you place faith in Jesus and establish Him as your Source of Life, only then can you move on to the second commandment which is to love others. Taking charge of my faith and family means I go into the world to care for others rather than reacting to them. If you find yourself caught up in one of the six cultural trends, start by asking this question: "Who or what is my source of life?"

There are some burdens that are too much for one person to carry. This is why we have family.

The answer to that question eliminates those conditional statements we listed earlier. Jesus as your Source of Life changes everything. When Jesus is the Source, you hear statements like:

"I will love my husband (wife) until death do us part."
"I will start by pursuing my wife's (husband's) heart."
"I forgive and honor my parents."
"I work as unto the Lord and view my job as a ministry."
"I love my church and will serve more than I expect others to serve."
"I won't wait for the government to make things easier for me. I will do the right thing no matter what."
"I will work hard, give much, save for the future, and spend wisely."

Those statements have power. Taking charge of your faith and family starts with you—not your church, spouse, parent, or child. Will you accept this responsibility? If so, I look forward to sharing with you in the chapters ahead how to guard your home, honor each other, work hard, form relationships, support the marriages and families around you, and support your church.

There are two sections at the end of each chapter to further discussion and thought on the subject. "Empowering Everyone in the Home" provides a summary and take-away for singles, spouses, and parents. "Family Conversation Starters" provides questions, fill-in-the-blanks, and activities to further discussion around the family table or in the car.

I'm often asked, "Ted, are you concerned, being a church that talks about marriage so much, that you're going to marginalize people?" That's a fair question, and it deserves an honest answer. Every time we talk about marriage and family we speak to three people in the application of the message. Our church desires to encourage singles, enrich spouses, and equip parents.

Encourage Singles

We desire to paint a beautiful picture of marriage for singles. We want them to see marriage as normative. We want them not to be afraid of it. For many singles, they come from a broken home and a healthy marriage was not modeled for them. We long for singles to esteem marriage as highly valuable. We want singles to understand also that they are backup singers to the duets all around them. We want singles to hear that their single friend is now engaged and not respond with "Are you sure? Don't ruin your life right now, so early. Slow down, take your time."

Enrich Spouses

Couples need to hear regularly that you don't need to choose between life and a spouse. You can enjoy both at the same time. Marital satisfaction involves skills and factors couples can do something about. Regular marriage and family teaching reminds couples that marriage takes daily decisions to move closer to and not away from each other.

Equip Parents

Topics such as compatibility, the kid-centered home, enjoying marriage, sexual intimacy, differences, and communication equip parents to disciple their children for future relationships and marriage. We seek to give Mom and Dad tools and conversation guides to help them be the first author of their child's heart. Relationship formation starts at home.

EMPOWERING EVERYONE IN THE HOME

Singles: Marriage should be honored by all. How do you respond when a friend begins to date and pursue marriage? Joy? Fear? Whatever model of marriage was on display for you during your childhood, search the Scripture and begin painting a beautiful picture of marriage that blesses the couples in your life and prepares you for your own marriage one day.

Spouses: A great marriage is a great gift for your children. Don't overlook your marriage as an incredible parenting skill. Guard your heart and don't give your affection to anyone other than your spouse. Prioritize marriage in the home.

Parents: Eradicate the kid-centered home. It's best for you and your children. Send your child out of the home as an adult, not on a journey to become one. Be the parent. Avoid burdening your child with the emotional pressure of being your companion.

FAMILY CONVERSATION STARTERS

1. Who is your source of life?

2. Has everyone in our home declared Jesus as the Source of Life?

3. How does a kid-centered home affect children as they become adults?

4. What are some ways we can prioritize marriage in the home?

5. What are some ways a single person honors marriage?

6. What can we do to encourage the marriages and families in our community and church?

7. Next time grandma and grandpa come over, ask them the following questions:

    - *How did you meet?*

    - *How long did you date before you knew you would marry?*

    - *What was your wedding like?*

    - *What was the most trying time of your marriage?*

CHAPTER 2

CATCHING FOXES

PRIORITIZING AND PROTECTING
MARRIAGE IN THE HOME

*"Integrity is keeping a commitment even
after circumstances have changed."*

—DAVID JEREMIAH

My wife and I are different in every way. I have a guilt-prone
OCD nature; she does not. I spend way too much time and
energy trying to please people. She lacks the people-pleasing gene.
I define savings as money you put away for a rainy day. She defines
savings as the difference between the actual price and the sale price.
I like to sleep with the house set at seventy-five degrees with a light
sheet covering us. She prefers sixty-nine point five degrees and a
thick comforter. She takes her coffee black. I need Coffee-mate.

All of these differences make marriage fun. Changing one
another is of no interest to us. We no longer strive for complete

agreement on every issue and opinion. Instead, we're deciding our way into enjoying life and marriage.

Marriage is all about decisions. The unspoken message of our culture is "Commitment and a divorce-proof marriage flows from character, but enjoyment flows from chemistry and compatibility." Great marriages flow from character, not chemistry. In a thriving marriage, character trumps chemistry every time. Character fuels powerful decisions, which grow a healthy home.

> *In a thriving marriage, character trumps chemistry every time. Character fuels powerful decisions, which grows a healthy home.*

Stop trying to change one another in the pursuit of happiness. Instead of changing your spouse's emotions, beliefs, opinions, personality, tastes, and decisions, what if you make the decision to enjoy life and your spouse? No matter how many challenges you face in life, decide to enjoy life and each other.

In Psalm 90:10, Moses stated that life is a grind:

> Our days may come to seventy years,
> or eighty, if our strength endures;
> yet the best of them are but trouble and sorrow,
> for they quickly pass, and we fly away.

The grind of life is difficult, brief, and at times painful. It doesn't matter how much money you make, you can't buy your way out of the grind. It doesn't matter how smart you are, you can't outsmart the grind. The grind hits us all.

In the midst of the grind, Solomon reminds us to enjoy life and marriage:

> "Go, eat your food with gladness, and drink your wine with a joyful heart, for God has already approved what you do. Always be clothed in white, and always anoint your head with oil. Enjoy life with your wife, whom you love, all the days of this meaningless life that God has given you under the sun—all your meaningless days. For this is your lot in life and in your toilsome labor under the sun." (Ecclesiastes 9:7–9)

Enjoying life and marriage has nothing to do with your education, finances, age, health, setbacks, or extended family members, but has everything to do with making powerful decisions. I don't choose the length or struggle of my toilsome labor under the sun, but I do choose to honor, prioritize, and enjoy marriage with my wife. I love and enjoy my wife!

IT'S CHARACTER, NOT CHEMISTRY

The decision to enjoy life and marriage flows from character, not chemistry. Amy and I made the decision eighteen years ago that divorce would never be an option. We made that decision and are sticking with it until either one of us lays the other in the arms of Jesus or He returns. The decision to enjoy life together flows from the same place. Enjoying marriage is a decision.

A few years ago Amy and I started keeping a list of all the reasons why we enjoy each other. We each have our own list. At the top of my list it says, "All of the reasons why it's fun loving Amy Cunningham." We shared our entire lists in the book, *Fun Loving You.*

My List for Amy Includes:

1. I love your "all or nothing" passion. You do nothing halfway. When you start a project, you finish it with gusto. You inspire me to work hard and get it done.

2. I love your disdain for directions. You love letting me lead. You couldn't care less how we are getting there. While driving or at airports, you pay no attention to signs because you completely trust me to get you there.

3. I love your selfless serving. From sunrise to sunset you never stop serving your family. Your family and friends are always comfortable when you serve them.

4. I love your adventurous culinary spirit. My favorite meal once was meat loaf, mashed potatoes, and corn. Not anymore. You have elevated my palate. Bring on the heat, spices, texture, and plating.

5. I love your confidence. You are secure in who you are as a wife and mom. This is one of your most attractive qualities.

Amy's List for Me Includes:

1. I love your implied questions that you deliver with strength. My favorite question is, "I look really good in this outfit, huh?"

2. I love that you're always concerned about my comfort when it comes to temperature. You constantly offer me your coat and even your socks when necessary.

3. I love how the child in you comes out when you get to build a fire. You get such a feeling of accomplishment, and it's displayed in your body language and on your face once the fire takes off.

4. I love your fiscal responsibility—the fact that you always know how much money I spent at Target before I even get home.

5. I love how easy you are to please. Whether we have cereal for dinner or filet mignon, you say, "That was a perfect dinner!"

Every frustration ends up on the list. The longer you're married the easier it is to just let things go. We tend to give up working through the differences. Too many couples just put up with each other rather than spotting things that need to be worked on and doing something about it.

Thriving marriages deteriorate if left alone. Healthy marriages require constant decision making. King Solomon used the word picture of a vineyard and foxes to describe potential destruction to the marriage:

"Catch for us the foxes,

the little foxes that ruin the vineyards,

our vineyards that are in bloom." (Song of Songs 2:15)

Marriage is a vineyard in bloom, and it needs time and protection to reach harvest. The big foxes are easy to spot; catching the little foxes requires scrutiny and diligence. The big foxes are what take you into counseling when all hope is lost. The big foxes ravage a vineyard quickly, if not overnight.

Healthy marriages require constant decision making.

In Solomon's day, stone walls protected the vineyard. It was easy to keep out the big foxes, but it took time to catch the little foxes. You had to walk around the wall looking for small holes or gaps in the gate that allowed the small foxes in. Over time, little foxes could eat away at the vineyard if the vintner didn't pay close attention.

I've never dealt with little foxes, but when we moved to the Ozarks, I dealt with another little critter that caused just as much damage. Shortly after moving into our home, we lay in bed one night catching up on the day. Just as we were about to drift off to sleep, a fluttering sound passed by our heads. We were quiet for a moment and then we heard it again.

Amy asked, "What was that?"

I, like most men, live by the philosophy that says, "If you act like you didn't hear it, it's not really there." The third time we heard the flapping noise, we also felt it.

Amy asked again, "What is it?"

I wanted to say, "I think it's a sparrow?" What I really said was, "Amy, I'm going to tell you what it is, but I need you to remain calm. I think it's a bat."

With a screech, under the covers she went. She took all the covers for herself, leaving me fully exposed to the bat. I jumped up and raced into the bathroom. I turned the lights on and peered through the crack in the door. I was safe.

Amy asked, "What are we going to do?!"

I said, "What are we going to do? I'm protected! *You* have a problem!" I caught my breath, then went back in to take care of the bat. What I did with the bat I will leave to your imagination.

We only lived in that house for eleven months. Moving had nothing to do with the bat. We wanted to downsize. Months later, our realtor called us to tell us the new owners had an exterminator come out to deal with a bat infestation. Uh-oh! Nothing good ever follows the word *infestation*.

We had no idea. We never went into the attic. The entry to the attic was sealed off and the inspection by the new owners at the time of sale didn't turn anything up either. We didn't disclose the bats because we had no idea they were up there.

Our realtor told us that they discovered over one hundred bats living in the attic. What? Their high-pitched screeches went unnoticed for over eleven months. All one hundred plus bats entered through very small holes in the soffit. That wasn't our only problem. There was a thick layer of fecal material on the floor of the attic. The bill for bat and fecal removal was around $1,500. We split it with the homeowners. All of that damage simply because we weren't diligent in looking for signs of trouble around our home.

We have many friends who never go in their crawl spaces or attics. That's a mistake. You want to catch the termites before you're faced with a $20,000 exterminator invoice. You want to know if mold is growing in the walls because of a leaky pipe or shower before a restoration company hands you a $5,000 bill for their services. If you catch it early, while it's small, you save yourself unnecessary destruction. What a great lesson for all of our relationships.

DEALING WITH THE FOXES

Do you have the courage to deal with the foxes in your marriage? Open and honest conversations about the foxes in your marriage vineyard can stave off disaster and destruction years down the road. Jesus dealt with the big foxes of murder and adultery in Matthew 5. He started by teaching that the big fox of murder starts small and in the heart:

> "You have heard that it was said to the people long ago, 'You shall not murder and anyone who murders will be subject to judgment.' But I tell you that anyone who is angry with a brother or sister will be subject to judgment." (vv. 21–22)

Deal with the anger in the heart before it leads to destruction like murder. If you are in a second marriage right now, that bitterness and resentment towards an ex-spouse is a little fox you need to deal with immediately. The anger and the frustration that you have with your parents is a little fox. I promise you that if you don't deal with it, if you don't resolve that anger, if you don't offer forgiveness, it will turn into a bigger issue and it will impact your marriage. A little fox won't destroy a vineyard overnight. As we walk around the vineyard, we want to spot early damage before the whole vineyard is destroyed. For some of you, you don't understand why being angry and hating your parents is a big deal, but it will destroy your marriage vineyard. It's a fox on the loose. It's a fox that you must deal with.

Jesus taught that adultery starts off as a little fox in the heart:

> "You have heard that it was said, 'You shall not commit adultery.' But I tell you that anyone who looks at a woman lustfully has already committed adultery with her in his heart." (vv. 27–28)

Amy was in bed one night, seven years into our marriage, reading a book on how men think. It's not a really thick book, you can read it in about a night. She asked, "Have you ever struggled with lust towards another woman?"

Men, let me teach you something. You start by acting as though you didn't hear the question. "What'd you say?"

"Have you ever struggled with lust towards another woman?"

Then you act as if you didn't understand the question. "What do you mean?"

I knew where this was headed. There was only one destination after an honest discussion. For a week, she mourned. She found discipleship and listened to everything she could. I can't tell you how many Beth Moore tapes we listened to. We talked and had painful conversations. Having that conversation about the little fox called lust was the greatest thing that ever happened in our marriage.

Amy said, "I will be your only fantasy." That's exclusivity. "Yes, ma'am!" I replied.

I don't want lust to destroy my marriage. That's why all my technology is available to my wife and children. I will not allow something like a cell phone, computer, or a cable channel to destroy my marriage. I just won't allow it. I love when the cable company calls and wants to give me certain channels for free. My response is simply, "No. I won't destroy my marriage with that channel. I won't let the little fox in." Not many telemarketers have heard that one.

> *Marriage is a vineyard in bloom that needs time and protection to reach harvest.*

Marriage is a vineyard in bloom that needs time and protection to reach harvest. Tending to it requires diligence and scrutiny. To enjoy the fine wine of matrimony, you need to catch the foxes that sneak in to nip the blooms and buds.

Simply stated, a fox is anyone or anything that seeks to destroy your marriage. Here are twenty more potential foxes to the vineyard of your marriage.

1. Bad Marriage Messaging.

Many pastors and leaders are at a loss about how to work with broken marriages in the church. Sometimes the problems seem too big and far reaching. We get louder and preach harder, but couples still break up and families fall apart. We must be clear, consistent, and hopeful in our messages and counseling to couples. Eliminate the messages with a negative tone like "God gave you your spouse to beat you down and suck the life out of you so you can be more like Jesus" and "Sex is dirty, nasty, and ugly, and you should save it for the one you love."

2. Children.

They are a blessing. We enjoy them and hope to stay close to them throughout their adult years. If we're not careful, it becomes all about them. Remember when good parents attended as many games as possible or as their work would allow? Now it seems the great parents attend *all* the practices and games. From practice to play dates, we spend our resources, energy, and time on the children only to give ourselves the leftovers. Mission Community Church in Phoenix, Arizona recently hosted a date night at the church for over 700 couples. Childcare was packed with over 400 kids. While the adults strengthened their marriages in the main auditorium, the children learned about marriage in the family life center. They studied the movements and strategies of the fox and were challenged with ways to avoid becoming a fox to their parents' marriage. I love it! We need to teach children how they can help to eradicate the kid-centered home.

3. Parents.

Enmeshed families trap both parents and adult children. Both parties share the responsibility of establishing firm boundaries so marriages thrive. You need to cut the strings relationally, emotionally, financially, and if necessary, geographically. Leave your family of origin and prioritize your new home.

4. Family and Friends.

I recently heard a pastor say, "There are voices in your life that you need to turn down, some you need to turn up, and some you need to mute altogether." Who in your family is planting seeds of doubt in your mind about your spouse? It may be time to hit the mute button on those who are bad backup singers to your marriage duet.

5. Social Media.

When I come home at night that is my time to disconnect and unwind. I disconnect from the world and relax with my family. The effects of Facebook, Twitter, Pinterest, and Instagram on mental, emotional, and relational health can be detrimental. Social media fills that leftover margin in our day. We come home at night and rest physically, unwind emotionally, disconnect relationally, relax mentally, and recharge spiritually. Instead we stay up late on our social-media outlets, comparing ourselves to others, connecting relationally, and stressing out over something clever to post.

It may be time to hit the mute button on those who are bad backup singers to your marriage duet.

Social media is one fox that not only has the potential to destroy a marriage vineyard, but can also sabotage a couple's chances for reconciliation. One desire of our church is to protect your family while your marriage is in crisis. One of our teaching pastors, Adam Donyes, worked with me to develop social media guidelines for separating, divorcing, and reconciling couples. As we pray and work towards reconciliation, we ask couples to consider these guidelines before posting anything online:

For the sake of my children, family and friends, I commit to the following guidelines when posting on social media:

1. I will not seek validation for my feelings through likes, comments, replies, or retweets.

2. I will only post that which is encouraging and edifying.

3. I refuse to vent or speak negatively about anyone or anything.

4. I will take personal responsibility by removing any posts that lead to negative comments. If it incites criticism towards my spouse, I will delete it.

5. I will avoid passive aggressive posting. For example, I will not post Bible verses that point to the actions or words of my spouse.

6. I will not post seductive pictures in an effort to "put myself out there."

7. I will not post pictures with a new boyfriend or girlfriend while my friends and family are still mourning the death of my marriage.

8. If I question a post, I will ask a mature friend to review it before I post.

9. I will not stalk the behavior of another via social media.

10. I will not create false accounts to manipulate, deceive, or act falsely towards someone else.

11. Above all, I will strive to use social media in a way that honors God, others, and my family, regardless of my feelings.

6. Past Relationships.

Unresolved hurt, fear, anger, bitterness, resentment, and rage from past relationships may sabotage your marriage. Bad breakups from the past often lead to mistrust.

7. Temptation.

Satan tempted Jesus, but Jesus did not sin. Temptation is not sin. We are all tempted in different ways. Establish financial, sexual, and relational boundaries and accountability with one another to avoid the pain and consequences of sin. I remember one pastor sharing with me, "Sin always takes you further than you want to go and keeps you longer than you ever planned to stay."

8. The "Look Out for Number One" Attitude.

Pride and selfishness lead to manipulation and destroys oneness. Be careful not to make your dreams, goals, and plans the priority. They are now "our dreams," "our goals," and "our plans."

9. Money.

The love of money can destroy your marriage. Avoid borrowing whenever possible: "The rich rule over the poor, and the borrower is slave to the lender" (Proverbs 22:7). Make sure that your use of credit does not replace your trust in God's timing—"Be still before the LORD and wait patiently for him; do not fret when people succeed in their ways, when they carry out their wicked schemes"

(Psalm 37:7). Avoid using credit when buying things you want, not things you need, and be content: "But godliness with contentment is great gain. For we brought nothing into the world, and we can take nothing out of it. But if we have food and clothing, we will be content with that" (1 Timothy 6:6–8). And pay your debts on time, for "the wicked borrow and do not repay, but the righteous give generously" (Psalm 37:21).

10. The American Dream.

The American Dream says you can be whoever you want and do whatever you want. The banks make it easy to achieve your dream with no money down and easy payments. All you need is a mortgage, car payments, and a time to pay it all off. Don't allow chasing material possessions and status in community to make your marriage shallow.

11. eHarmony and Match.com Commercials.

I've always been a horrible test-taker, and I don't believe a test guarantees someone's ability to remain faithful for life. These commercials are geared towards singles, but think for a minute about the spouse in a stuck marriage watching one of those commercials. The spouse sees a couple twirling around on the screen, smiling, and holding hands and begins to think, *I would like to enjoy life like that, but there's no way I can experience that in this marriage.* Compatibility is not something you find, test for, or stumble into. Daily decisions that flow from your character create compatibility over the long haul.

12. Bad Counseling.

The marriage counselor may be "LMFT" (Licensed Marriage and Family Therapist), but that doesn't mean he or she will advocate for your marriage with sound biblical advice. Beware! Bad counseling dishonors marriage. Healthy counseling builds up marriage.

13. Age and Attitude.

Don't allow aging and the difficulty associated with it diminish your marriage. Ecclesiastes 12:1 says, "Remember your Creator in the days of your youth, before the days of trouble come and the years approach when you will say, 'I find no pleasure in them.'" I love watching people grow old and sweet at the same time. I love watching senior couples hold hands and enjoy one another's company. As your body finds its way into the grind, don't let your attitude follow.

While writing this book, my dear friend and mentor Gary Smalley was fighting for his life. On July 31, 2014, he had seven-bypass open-heart surgery. Months later, we continue to pray that God will get his heart, liver, and kidneys working again. It's been a very tough road.

Two months after the surgery, I went to see Gary in Colorado Springs and spent the day walking around the hospital with him as he endured many tests and procedures. Multiple times throughout the day he said, "Say something funny and make me laugh." I responded with, "I will not be responsible for your death." That did the trick. He laughed.

Gary Smalley has the best attitude in a seventy-four-year-old body I have ever seen. I mean, he loves his Lord and family and doesn't allow his struggle and pain to get to his attitude. May this be true of each one of us and our marriages.

14. Statistics and Research.

Don't be frightened by statistics. I have many friends passionate about studying research and data. They are wise enough to filter studies and stats through the filter of God's Word. Truth trumps trends. Don't allow the overused and inaccurate stat of a 50 percent divorce rate scare you out of marriage. Don't use it as an excuse. My friend Shaunti Feldhahn has dispelled the myth of the "50 percent divorce rate" stat in her book *The Good News About Marriage: Debunking Discouraging Myths About Marriage and Divorce.* The best takeaway from Shaunti's message is that your chances for divorce decrease significantly if you plug into a church and attend with great regularity.

15. Duty and Responsibility.

Be very careful not to allow duty and responsibility to trump curiosity and fascination. Paying bills, working a job, maintaining a house, and raising kids can create a vacuum of intimacy in your marriage. We must not neglect these duties, but we must create enough margin to keep the spark fresh and the relationship on fire.

16. Unemployment.

I've watched couples struggle because one or both refuse to work. There are many reasons for this. Sometimes that spouse is waiting for a job in their field of interest. You may need to work any job until the perfect job comes along. Laziness is a character issue. When you combine a strong work ethic with competency and skills, income follows. In chapter 5, we'll see how the principles of work directly relate to the success of relationships in the home.

17. Ministry and Serving.

Even good things can turn bad in the best of marriages. Your church has a lot to offer and has many needs for volunteers. Serving the Lord is critically important in your walk with Christ. Don't wear yourself down and neglect your family. You may need to say no to the greater yes.

18. Trials.

Your marriage will face hardships, and you must choose whether you will allow those hardships to be foxes. Paul says that suffering produces character (Romans 5:3–4), and James tells us to "consider it pure joy, my brothers, whenever you face trials of many kinds, because you know that the testing of your faith develops perseverance" (James 1:2). Trials are not intended to destroy the Christian; instead, God uses them to make us more like Jesus. Learn from trials without turning on each other. Lean into each other as you go through trials.

19. Boredom.

Comedian Chris Rock said, "You really only have two choices in life. You can be single and lonely or married and bored." Wrong! I believe marriage should be enjoyed. According to Ecclesiastes 9:7–9, you should sit down for a nice meal and enjoy your spouse.

20. The Grind.

God gave you your spouse to go through the grind with you, not to become part of it. You know you have made them a part of the grind when their words start sounding like something coming from Charlie Brown's teacher: "Womp-womp, womp-womp,

womp-womp." Go through the grind together as teammates, not as opponents.

Lean into each other as you go through trials.

Small things have the potential for becoming big things. For years, I've watched spouses use small things as justification for divorce. These simple excuses are best described as trivial.

In Matthew 19:3, the Pharisees referenced trivial excuses when they questioned Jesus: "Is it lawful for a man to divorce his wife for any and every reason?" We hear many of these "for any and every reason" excuses today.

A few years ago I started writing down all the trivial reasons people give for divorce. These excuses are in no way related to abuse or infidelity. These are the trivial and unbiblical excuses used to justify a way out of a boring, passionless, frustrating, hurtful, or stuck marriage. When we meditate on these thoughts they form beliefs. These beliefs are foxes:

1. No one will understand, so I won't bother explaining.

2. I want to be happy.

3. I can't be happy with him/her.

4. I've put up with this long enough.

5. God knows I've tried to make this marriage work.

6. God wants me to be happy.

7. We're just not compatible.

8. We have no chemistry.

9. We have nothing in common.

10. We have no sexual chemistry.

11. He/she no longer finds me attractive.

12. We've tried everything to get along.

13. I've tried everything to get along.

14. It's a two-way street, and he/she won't meet me halfway.

15. He/she has changed.

16. He/she won't change.

17. He/she never left home.

18. He/she has been depressed for years.

19. He/she has a mental health issue.

20. Everyone says I deserve better.

21. We never should've married in the first place.

22. He/she should be single.

23. Marriage isn't for everyone.

24. God would rather we divorce before a murder takes place.

25. God has someone out there better for my spouse.

26. It would be better for the kids.

27. There's someone out there better for me.

28. There's someone out there better for him/her.

29. I can't love him/her like I should.

30. We have fallen out of love.

31. In God's eyes, we were never really married.

32. With time, people will see that this decision is right.

33. I give up.

34. We have too many issues that will never be resolved.

35. She/he spends too much money.

36. Our counselor says our marriage can't be saved.

37. There's too much water under the bridge.

38. I can't forgive.

39. We'll never be able to move past (name the issue).

40. We need to go our separate ways.

41. We can divorce but stay friends for the kids' sake.

42. We've lived too many years like this; we need some room to breathe.

43. I found someone new.

44. No one gets what I'm going through.

45. God hasn't called me to live a celibate life.

46. It's not me; it's him/her.

47. We both want this.

48. I know it's wrong, but God will forgive me.

49. I want to be alone.

50. I'm not meant to be a married person.

What thoughts have become foxes in your marriage? A negative narrative is a string of thoughts that you repeat to yourself over long periods of time. If you repeat a lie long enough, you'll eventually convince yourself that it's true. It's time to change the narrative of your marriage and chase out the negative thoughts and foxes.

I met a sweet couple in Iowa City, Iowa, a few years back. He told me, "Ted, don't stop doing what you're doing. You keep it going." His name is Lloyd. He cheered me on in my passion to encourage couples.

I said, "You betcha, Lloyd, I will."

He said, "Everything you're saying is true!"

I love asking guys like Lloyd who have been married a few decades to tell me the secret to a smokin' hot marriage. Lloyd told me a story I'll never forget.

Back in the 1940s, he was smitten with a young lady named Jean. He said, "Ted, I was head over heels. I wanted to marry her, but I had to go to war."

While at war, he wrote Jean almost every day from his bunker. Most of his writing was at night. He said, "Let me tell you something. Everything was on the table. I put all of my thoughts and all of my heart out there for Jean. There was no thought hidden. I just poured out what I was thinking and feeling."

Before he left for war, they chose a star that shined above the Big Dipper as "their" star. As they wrote their letters at night, they would occasionally look to the star. It brought them comfort to know that on opposite sides of the world they both watched the star.

Writing letters during World War II was the sole source of communication with loved ones. There was a whole department of the military that would read every soldier's letter and edit out details that could give away secrets or locations.

Lloyd showed me one of his boxes of letters to Jean from WWII. The box contained hundreds of edited letters. He said, "This is our life. There was no stone left unturned. We talked about it all."

Before Jean and Lloyd were married in 1944, they spent the war years tending to their marriage vineyard. They have been married now for seventy years. Lloyd walks with Jesus and loves his wife.

As I said goodbye to this sweet couple, Jean reached into her purse and pulled out two folding canes. Like Indiana Jones, they both whipped their canes straight and headed for the parking lot hand in hand. Later that day, I told Amy we're getting a pair of those canes. Lord willing, I hope to make it to seventy years of marriage. I want a harvest like Lloyd and Jean.

WHY PRIORITIZE AND PROTECT MARRIAGE?

On the second Sunday morning of every month, our church teaches on marriage and family. The goal is to inspire singles, spouses, and parents with a healthy view of marriage and family by taking charge of their lives. We call it Twolgnite Sunday and use three words to guide the messaging: *honor, enjoy,* and *prioritize.*

Honor.

Hebrews 13:4 states, "Marriage should be honored by all, and the marriage bed kept pure, for God will judge the adulterer and all the sexually immoral." At first glance we tend to focus on the "marriage bed kept pure." To do so overlooks the clear teaching that each of us must lift high the institution of marriage. Honor decides. It makes a decision to esteem marriage as highly valuable. God didn't ordain marriage to be a miserable weight you endure in order to grow closer to Him. Our goal with honor is to paint a beautiful and desirable picture of marriage and family for every single person in our congregation.

Enjoy.

Ecclesiastes 9:7–9 says to "go, eat your food with gladness, and drink your wine with a joyful heart, for it is now that God favors what you do. Always be clothed in white, and always anoint your head with oil. Enjoy life with your wife, whom you love, all the

The bond between husband and wife is meant to be permanent this side of heaven.

days of this meaningless life that God has given you under the sun—all your meaningless days. For this is your lot in life and in your toilsome labor under the sun."

Life is difficult, yes, and you don't have complete control over the events and circumstances that life throws at you. However, you can decide to enjoy each other. You can't escape the grind, but for goodness' sake, don't turn your spouse into the grinder. God didn't give you your spouse as part of the grind. God gave you your spouse to go through the grind with you. You don't have to choose between life and a spouse. You can enjoy life with your spouse in the midst of the grind.

Prioritize.

In the midst of the grind you must prioritize your marriage in the home. The kid-centered home isn't good for your marriage or the kids. Genesis 2:24 is a parenting and marriage verse that prioritizes marriage: "For this reason a man will leave his father and mother and be united to his wife, and they will become one flesh." The bond between husband and wife is meant to be permanent this side of heaven. That's not the bond we have with our children. Your children will not be with you forever, so start planning and preparing for their departure sooner rather than later.

When we honor, enjoy and prioritize marriage in the church and home, we eradicate the kid-centered home and bless our children with the gift of Mom and Dad enjoying life together.

When we honor, enjoy, and prioritize marriage in the church and home, we bring our children out of adolescence and send them out of the home as an adult, not on a journey to become one.

When we honor, enjoy, and prioritize marriage in the church and home, we eliminate the fear and unnecessary delay of marriage in our children.

When we honor, enjoy, and prioritize marriage in the church and home, we form healthy relationships by making decisions that build commitment.

When we honor, enjoy, and prioritize marriage in the church and home, couples and families find hope in Jesus. He breathes life into dead people and dead couples. (Let's pray for more relationship updates on Facebook that read "Reconciled!")

When we honor, enjoy, and prioritize marriage in the church and home, our senior adults will continue to be examples of commitment, loyalty, duty, responsibility, and longevity.

EMPOWERING EVERYONE IN THE HOME

Singles: It's never too early to take charge of your future vineyard. Start with your beliefs on marriage. What you have seen and heard over your lifetime has formed beliefs in your heart about what marriage looks like. Align your beliefs with Scripture. In the final chapter we will examine marriage beliefs according to Scripture.

Spouses: Take charge of the foxes in your souls. Ask the Lord to search your hearts for anything that has the potential to cause damage to your marriage over the years. If both spouses feel safe and willing, discuss the obvious foxes and what can be done to chase them out of the vineyard.

Parents: How will you respond when your child expresses feelings of love for the first time? Will you rejoice, delight, and praise God for the feelings He placed inside your child? Before you get to know the one for whom the affections flow, start by validating what God does in each of us emotionally. After you validate the feelings (Song of Songs 1:4), then guide them to not arouse or awaken love before its time (Song of Songs 2:7).

FAMILY CONVERSATION STARTERS

1. Spend a few moments watching some YouTube clips on the behavior of foxes. Make this fun.

2. Discuss some obvious ways marriages deteriorate and end up in divorce.

3. What foxes are in your marriage vineyard?

4. What can children do to help parents guard the vineyard (and keep from becoming foxes themselves)?

5. What excuses for divorce have you heard from family and friends?

CHAPTER 3

HONORING ROLES

ACCEPTING AND APPRECIATING
EVERY PERSON IN THE FAMILY

*"When we honor someone we give that person a
highly respected position in our lives."*

—GARY SMALLEY

D r. Gary Smalley has taught me much over the past thirteen
years. His wisdom bleeds through our entire ministry to
marriages and families. By far, his Honor List is the greatest tool
for esteeming those you love as highly valuable.

A few years ago he showed me four pages of a bulleted list.
Each bullet was a statement of high honor for his wife, Norma
Smalley. I asked him, "What do you do with this list?"

"If Norma and I have a disagreement with one another, I
pull this list out and begin reading what I wrote," he answered.
The goal wasn't to cross things off the list that he didn't believe
anymore. Instead, it was to remind himself of Norma's incredible

> *Each member of the family uniquely bears the image of God to the world.*

value. This is referred to as *confirmation bias,* making decisions then looking for the evidence to back them up. Gary decided Norma was highly valuable. Reading the list was like gathering evidence of her worth. That is truly beautiful!

This teaching has been the anchor of Gary's ministry over the past forty years. So much so that he produced a magazine called *Homes of Honor.* Every member of the family is highly valuable. Healthy families spend their days looking for the evidence to back up that value.

Why do we have value? The answer is simple. God created us in His image. That gives us automatic, intrinsic value. Our worth comes from God, not others.

Each member of the family uniquely bears the image of God to the world. Mom bears the image of a nurturing God. Dad bears the image of an ever-present Father. Children bear the image of a life-giving God.

HOW DOES MOM BEAR THE IMAGE OF GOD TO THE WORLD?

The week before Mother's Day 2014, I went on Facebook and asked folks to tell me about their moms. I asked them to complete this sentence: "My mom is _____."

- Nancy wrote: My mom is *the best mom on the planet!* My mom is fun-loving, joyful, my prayer warrior, my number one cheerleader, a gift from God, and I love her so very much.

- Katie wrote: My mom is unwavering truth and grace. She knows the truth because of her relationship with Jesus and she is not afraid to stand for it, but she is also a soft place to land, full of grace, when we don't choose to follow the truth. She then reminds us of the truth not so softly and we love her for it.

- Anna wrote: My mom is supercalifragilisticexpialidocious.

- Joanna wrote: My mom is lucky. I'm kidding, my mom is kind-hearted and nurturing. and I'm proud to call her Mom.

- Angela wrote: My mom is a selfless woman, strong and courageous in the Lord, and a blessing to all who know her.

- Nann wrote: My mom is a wonderful example of grace and mercy. She could have knocked my block off, but she didn't.

- Joann wrote: My mom is eighty-three years old, and she is the energizer bunny. She keeps going and going and going.

- Shauna wrote: My mom is a crazy woman whom I respect, admire, adore, and hope to be like some day.

- Doug wrote: My mom is an example to others of how to be a loving mother who is Christlike. I'm so blessed to have her as my mom.

- Kristin wrote: My mom is a celebrator.

- Josh wrote: My mom is the bomb.

- Amy wrote: My mom is unselfish.

- Brandy wrote: My mom is a constant reminder of what kind of mom I strive to be.

- Paula wrote: My mom is my prayer warrior.

- Sundi Jo wrote: My mom is one of the first people in her family to use the words "I love you."

- Lori wrote: My mom is a godly woman, my close friend, my sounding board, my go-to person.

It just does something wonderful to my heart to hear children praise their moms. When we bless our moms, something happens in the hearts of the person blessing and the person blessed. You can't go wrong with honor.

Proverbs 30:17 teaches, "The eye that mocks a father, that scorns an aged mother, will be pecked out by the ravens of the valley, will be eaten by the vultures." This is a great bedtime verse. It's a word picture for death and teaches us how important it is to respect parents. Respect for authority begins at home. Before the boss, school teacher, or college professor, Mom is the first one to teach us respect and honor.

To give you an example, do you have an athlete whom you respect and would love to meet and spend some time with? Maybe it's an actor, artist, or musician? For me, it's not really actors, musicians, or athletes. Believe it or not, I fumble over my words and struggle when in the presence of older, wiser pastors. I've met Rick

Warren twice and both times could not put two sentences together. The thumbprint of his ministry is all over the church I pastor.

I tagged along on a ministry trip with Gary Smalley to Saddleback Church in 2005. I knew Pastor Rick was out of town, but I thought a trip to the "mothership" would be fun.

When we arrived on campus, Gary went straight to Pastor Rick's office and asked if he could look around. Gary is a bold adventurer, hindered by nothing. The receptionist gave him the go ahead.

As Gary looked at the books on the shelf behind Pastor Rick's desk, he turned and noticed me standing at the threshold of the door.

"What are you doing? Get in here," he insisted. I shook my head and didn't budge.

I can't explain it, but Pastor Rick's office gripped me with respect and timidity. It was fear . . . the good kind of fear.

Gary laughed and asked, "Do you want to sit at his desk?" He knew that was out of the question.

Why do I get this way around pastors? It's because I esteem them as highly valuable.

When you're in the presence of your parents, what feelings come over you? Reverence? Appreciation? Sadness? Hurt? Frustration? Is your desire to put your parents down or build them up? Do you remind them of all their

> We must esteem our parents as highly valuable.

failures, mistakes, and everything they did wrong? How I treat my parents sets the course for my faith and family. We must esteem our parents as highly valuable. I can't think of a better place to start than with Mom.

THE HIGH VALUE OF MOM

A few summers ago at a family camp I taught on the subject of honor. I challenged the adults to make an honor list for their parents. We started with five reasons why Mom is highly valued. The goal was to email, mail, or phone the list to mom.

After that morning's teaching, a woman approached me and said, "You told us to write down five reasons why mom is valuable. I can't think of one." She was not in a good spot. Her tone showed her hurt, frustration, and anger.

I backed up a little bit and asked, "If you can't think of five right now, can you start with one?"

That sparked a list of reasons why her mom was a fool for living a destructive lifestyle. Validating her pain was all I could do. Through tears she shared story after story of her mom's immaturity.

I pointed her to what should be at the top of everyone's honor list for mom: "Thank you for giving birth to me." Each one of us is here because of our mother. God "knit me together in my mother's womb" (Psalm 139:13). This tops the list.

Mom does so much more than give life. My mom taught me how to tie my shoes and brush my teeth. She taught me how to read. She taught me how to type. The first time I asked about sex, she gave honest answers to my direct questions. She held nothing back. Mom was my first teacher.

There is no perfect mom. Like most, she loses her patience and gets frustrated. She tires after long days and says things she regrets. Choose to let that go and build her up for her relentless care of you.

On Mother's Day 2014, we handed every member of our church and guest a greeting card as they walked into worship. On the outside of the card it simply read, "Mom's Honor List." On the inside there were five bullets "1, 2, 3, 4, and 5." We asked each member and guest to fill out this card and give it to their mom that week. Better yet, we suggested that each person go to their mom and read it to her. If that wasn't possible, we asked them to pick up the phone and call. Here are a few of the lists some of our members shared before the entire congregation:

Shay Robbins wrote to his mom, Susan Robbins:

1. She taught us how to make life an adventure.

2. She was and is a constant source of encouragement, love, and admiration; she has always made me feel special.

3. She believes in her husband and children and celebrates our accomplishments.

4. She makes wonderful pies.

5. She gives us enough room to make our mistakes and is the first one there to comfort us through life's hard lessons.

Dave Rogers wrote to his mom, Carolyn Rogers:

1. My mom taught me resilience and mental toughness. God grants us strength when we need it most; not before and not after, but during a crisis or problem. God made my mom tough.

2. My mom taught me loyalty. Stand by your man. Disagree in private. My mom never argued with Father in front of us. She always supported her husband. Trust me; there were times, like when we used machetes to thin the frog population in our yard. She disagreed with Dad allowing this, but she went with it.

3. My mom is persistent. Never give up on your kids. I gave her plenty of reasons to bail, but she didn't. She prayed, loved, and encouraged me, without condoning or condemning.

4. My mom is an encourager; the right amount at the right time. My mom lets me know she is proud of me when I do something that deserves praise. She has demonstrated the value of looking for those moments of emotional investments in those around me.

5. My mom taught me compassion. Take action when your internal trigger is pulled. Over the years I've watched my mom go to someone who needed a hug or a touch and quietly minister to them. This is the greatest gift she has given me.

Sashanna Caldwell wrote to her mom, Beth Stephan:

1. My mom truly loves the Lord, desires to follow Him, and wants to be changed by Him. I am blessed by her relationship with the Lord. She has shown me

how our relationships with God are a process, and she continues to grow and change, which is very encouraging to me as a new mom.

2. Mom is crazy about Dad; enough said.

3. Mom has shown me the value of being present in her children's lives from infancy through adulthood. Her relationships with us have grown as we have become more intentional.

4. Mom has opened our home to all types of hurting people. We bring our friends home from college, from our jobs, from our adult lives, and she makes them feel like part of our family. She, along with Dad of course, have made our home into a haven for all types of people. Friends from college, ten years later, are still talking about the impact our home had on their lives. That's because Mom made it home for everyone.

5. Mom taught me the value of being adventurous, crazy, intentional, and extravagant in love.[7]

We ended our Mother's Day morning by remembering all the moms who were with the Lord. We received just as many responses from people speaking of their moms who are no longer here. This list brings me to tears every time I read it.

• Christopher, Susan, Kevin, and Sandy all responded with: My mom is with Jesus.

- Mark wrote: My mom is missed every day, yet her legacy lives on.

- Ann wrote: My mom is celebrating her first Mother's Day with the Lord.

- Patty wrote: My mom is in heaven with my dad; however, while I got to share my time with her here on the earth, my mom is the best, period.

- Jen wrote: My mom is celebrating her birthday and Mother's Day for the first time with Jesus.

- Erica wrote: My mom is terribly missed. I wish she were still here because I have all of these things that I want to share with her.

- Connie wrote: My mom is missed. She was a wonderful mom, and I was blessed to have her for the first thirty-two years of my life. The last fourteen years have been a learning experience, and I thank God for teaching me how to move on. Thank you, Lord.

- Sean wrote: My mom is gone too soon.

- Teri wrote: My mom is gone, but not forgotten. She worked hard, asked for little, and sacrificed for others.

- Kari wrote: My mom is in heaven, but always a servant of Christ.

- Marty wrote: My mom is at peace with no pain, no cancer, no worries. She is missed here on earth, but she is with Jesus to whom she committed her life and worshipped even through the pain. This is my tenth Mother's Day without her.

- Dave wrote: My mom is waiting for me.

- Linda wrote: My mom is in heaven, sheltered in the arms of God. This is my first Mother's Day without her.

- William wrote: My mom is gloriously in the presence of the Almighty Lord and Creator of all things.

My mom, Bonnie Cunningham, wrote the longest post: "My mom is with Jesus. I'm blessed to have had her with me for sixty-five years here and will miss talking to her this Sunday. Every day, I wish I could pick up the phone and hear her voice of encouragement; my biggest fan. Everyone wanted her for their mom. Blessed she was mine. We have a plan to meet at the eastern gate one day. She told me the last time I was with her that it's going to be very crowded at that gate. She was always such a card."

When I shared these honor lists with my son, I asked him, "Where should we take the Pamas (a.k.a. grandmas) for Mother's Day to read them their honor lists?"

Without hesitation, Carson said, "Let's take them to Disney World." I had been thinking more along the lines of Cracker Barrel.

THE HIGH VALUE OF DAD

As I grow older, I forget details of stories. I tell our congregation all the time, "That just helps my creativity." Even though I forget details, the lessons in the stories stick with me.

I was around nine years old, when my dad and I took an evening trip to Kmart. My dad wanted to get a country music album. I can't remember the artist or the car we drove, but I'll never forget what happened.

My dad has never been the type of guy who enjoys spending money on himself. When you look up "frugal" or "thrifty" in the dictionary, it should say, "Ron Cunningham." So it shocked me that he splurged on this album. As we sat in the car after the purchase, Dad counted his change and looked at the receipt. He discovered that the cashier had given him too much change. He said, "Wait here." He went back inside the store to settle the account and give back the excess change. Dad is a model of integrity.

Focus on the Family recently released a curriculum titled *The Family Project.* I watched all twelve sessions of this curriculum in three days. It caught my attention and never lost it. In the "Fathers as Image Bearers" session they share, "The presence and participation of the father changes everything." Children need fathers. Dads provide safety and security in the home.

I may be present in the home, but what is my participation level? Am I an engaged dad or an observing dad? I think most dads relate to being exhausted and "checked out" from the family, even when they are at home. As I heard Pastor Tommy Nelson say years ago, "When dad goes passive, the home goes dead." Making a living and taking care of a family is stressful, but I never want that to be an excuse for being an observing dad. We dads must engage in our homes.

Why is this so important? It's important because Dad exemplifies our relationship with our heavenly Father. Ephesians 6:4 puts it this way: "Fathers, do not exasperate your children;

instead, bring them up in the training and instruction of the Lord." I like how Eugene Peterson puts this in his paraphrase of *The Message*. He says, "Fathers, don't exasperate your children by coming down hard on them. Take them by the hand and lead them in the way of the Master."

Children need fathers. Dads provide safety and security in the home.

I have a son and a daughter. My daughter holds my hand all the time, and she still calls me Daddy. She's eleven years old. She knows I love her calling me daddy and never want that to change.

Carson is a different story. He's my boy, and his attitude is: "We fight together, Dad." I'm his karate practice partner. I'm the one he elbows and knees. This is how we bond. He's not a hand-holder unless we're in a crowd. When we're surrounded by tall people, he automatically reaches for my hand. More than simply not provoking our children to wrath, that verse in Ephesians encourages us to guide them daily through our participation and presence in the home.

The Family Project also teaches that, "A father is an image of divine authority. Our earthly dad paints a picture for us (in word and deed) of our heavenly Father."

Dad's role goes way beyond just providing for the family and participating in the home. He represents authority by establishing and enforcing boundaries. He gets to be the heavy in the home.

A few years back I walked into our family room while the kids watched television and said, "All right, I'm bringing the hammer down. Your mom needs some help around here and it's time to minimize privilege and maximize responsibility. Turn the TV off, pick up your clothes, take the dishes to the kitchen, make your beds, then ask mom what else needs to be done."

They immediately jumped up and went about their chores. While picking up his clothes, Carson said to Amy, "Dad said if we don't pick up these clothes he's going to hit us in the head with a hammer." He took my statement a bit out of context.

Dad's presence and participation in the home provide a model for children to follow. Our children see everything we do and hear everything we say. Their tendency is to repeat what they see and hear.

Jerry Buckley is an accountant in our church and a good friend of my dad's. I ran into him one day at lunch and he asked me, "Did you know your dad still does his own taxes?"

I said, "Yeah, and I'm assuming he still does it at the kitchen table with a blue Bic pen." He will never switch over to Turbo Tax.

The funny thing is, I do my own taxes at the kitchen table with a blue pen. The only difference is I use a gel pen, not a Bic. People think I'm crazy, but my taxes are simple. I've been paying taxes since I was twelve years old. Isn't it something how much we pick up from watching our parents over the years? You don't even realize it. It shouldn't surprise you that I also vote for the same candidates that Ron Cunningham votes for.

Let's look at some examples of how an earthly dad paints a picture of our heavenly Father. It goes two ways. Norman Wright does a beautiful job explaining for all of us the different ways an earthly dad can paint such a picture:

> If your father was a pushy man who was inconsiderate
> of you, or who violated and used you, you may see God
> in the same way. You probably feel cheap or worthless

in God's eyes, and perhaps feel that you deserve to be taken advantage of by others.

If your father was like a drill sergeant, demanding more and more from you with no expression of satisfaction, or burning with anger with no tolerance for mistakes, you may have cast God in his image.

If your father was a weakling, and you couldn't depend on him to help you or defend you, your image of God may be that of a weakling. You may feel that you are unworthy of God's comfort and support, or that He is unable to help you.

If your father was overly critical and constantly came down hard on you, or if he didn't believe in you or your capabilities and discouraged you from trying, you may perceive God in the same way. You don't feel as if you're worth God's respect or trust.

If your father was patient, you are more likely to see God as patient and available for you. You feel that you are worth God's time and concern.

If your father was a giving man, you may perceive God as someone who gives to you and supports you. You feel that you are worth God's support and encouragement.

If your father accepted you, you tend to see God accepting you regardless of what you do.

If your father protected you, you probably perceive God as your protector in life. [8]

What picture did your dad paint for you? What picture are you painting for your children?

Father's Day is one month after Mother's Day. Our church so loved the Honor List Mother's Day card that we decided to do the same thing for our dads. Sure, you could go to Target or Walmart and buy a card with words someone else wrote, but personalizing honor goes further with your father.

Here are a few honor lists from members at our church.

- Nancy Ellis wrote to her dad, Frank Kitchens:

Being one of daddy's girls and the baby of the family, I looked up to you. I've always been proud to say you're my father. You taught us young to be honest at all costs, to work hard, especially when no one was looking, and to give of self. You showed us that giving is not all about money in life, but what you can do and give of self, to and for others. That's what counts. My most valuable lessons were learned not by words, but by your actions. One was to love until death do us part and mean it. Even when Mom had Alzheimer's for years, you never left her side, but cared for her every need in our home until the day the Lord came for her. But the most important thing you taught me was to have a relationship with Christ and not just practice religion. We love you, Dad.

- Carla Bradley wrote her favorite things about her dad, Carl Kelly:

1) You have displayed unwavering, unconditional love through the years.

2) You model contentment.

3) You provided for us and taught us the value of integrity and work while you were raising us.

4) You care for your grandchildren. Watching you light up in their youth gives me a glimpse of how you were with me when I was a young child.

5) Your fashion sense improves with age. (No more Roman gladiator tire-tread sandals.)

• Savannah Sinclair wrote her favorite things about her dad, Joe Sinclair:

1) You are an amazing role model to me. You are definitely a man I look up to. You show me how a man should treat me and you walk the talk which I think are two very important things to teach your kid.

2) You are a great listener. I can tell you anything, and you will always be there for me with open arms and will listen.

3) You live your life to the fullest. In your life, there is never a dull moment. You always do something whether it's playing poker with your friends or volunteering at church. You're always going.

4) You are very selfless. You think of everyone but yourself. Just to name a few: you are always doing things around the house, you volunteer at our church, and you're always buying little gifts for everybody.

5) You support me and my mom too. I would have to say that you are my biggest fan. You are involved in my life and you support me in everything I do. [9]

THE HIGH VALUE OF CHILDREN

When our drummer at church and his wife were expecting their first child, I called them up to the stage one Sunday morning and presented them with a suitcase. It was a reminder that children are not with us forever and the entire family needs to plan accordingly. Children leave home eventually and until they do, we are packing their suitcase with what they need to survive.

The suitcase reminds us to be intentional about what we are packing. The days go slowly, but the years go fast. How we value the time says much about how we value our children.

Focus on the Family's *The Family Project* makes this beautiful declaration: "Every child is a bold proclamation from God that He stills desires to uniquely reveal Himself to the world through each of us." God is the creator and sustainer of all life. When a child is born, we witness the miracle of life granted to us by our Creator!

This is why Jesus valued children. When you turn to Matthew 19:14 you read, "Jesus said, 'Let the little children come to me, and do not hinder them, for the kingdom of heaven belongs to such as these.'" The heading in your Bible over that verse might say, "Jesus Welcomed Children." We picture a smiling Jesus sitting on a rock, placing a child on His lap. The Scripture says He became indignant and angry when the disciples kept children from Him. The disciples were swept up in the Greco-Roman culture of the day, which taught children were insignificant. Childhood at the time was considered an insignificant season of life. When Jesus welcomed a child, He made a huge statement of value. His actions boldly proclaimed, "Children are super important in the kingdom of God!"

Do you value children? Okay, let me ask you in a different way. Do you value a screaming child? *Confirmation bias* is a term we use in marriage counseling. This bias makes decisions then looks for the evidence to back them up. A frustrated husband with the negative narrative in his head that says, "My wife is a nag," only hears nagging words. A frustrated wife with the negative narrative "My husband is lazy," only sees his napping and lounging.

The same thing is true with children. It hit me a few years ago when our family went out to dinner with our friends the Watsons. Stephanie Watson is our children's director at Woodland Hills and our families have a fun time when together. I've always enjoyed the company of Roy and Sam, her two sixteen-year-old sons. When our families are together, we need a table for ten.

On this particular evening, something happened that I was oblivious to, but not Stephanie. There was an older woman sitting next to us who scowled at us through dinner. Apparently, teenagers having an appropriately good time was not something she favored. She directed her scowls towards Sam and Roy. I didn't fully understand it, but it was the very first time I saw through the eyes of a mom. I probed further into the situation.

Stephanie said, "Ted, this happens all the time. We walk into a place, and people see two teenage boys and automatically assume they're up to no good."

Children leave home eventually and until they do, we are packing their suitcase with what they need to survive.

How about a mom with a two-year-old? How many times in the grocery store have you avoided an aisle with a screaming child? I have. A two-year-old should know better, right? Do you know why two-year-olds act out? It's because they are transitioning from non-communicators to communicators. Their vocabulary is limited. This is Parenting 101. When I want something I say, "I would like that please." Without a vocabulary, a two-year-old screams, "Whahhhhhhhhh!"

As a follower of Jesus, to value and welcome children you don't need to sit on a rock and have children sit on your lap. Just imagine what might happen if the next time you saw a young mom struggling with a screaming child, you blessed her and the child by saying, "Mom, you're doing a great job! Keep at it!"

Maybe the next time you're on a plane and a mom with a small child sits next to you, instead of reaching for your Bose headphones, why not engage the child? Instead of thinking, *Shut that screaming kid up!* see if you can get a playful response from the child. Grandparents are pros at this. This interaction proclaims value.

While we're on the subject of screaming children, we must address the subject of crying babies in church. I have pastor friends and church members on both sides of this issue. So whether your response is, "Get that baby out of here" or "Oh, how precious, we have a baby in the service," let's look at it through the lens of high value.

Does your church value children? I can hear one of my pastor friends' answer to that question, "Yes I do, but in the nursery."

Persistent crying in a church service doesn't bother me. I'm not as distracted by it as I used to be. It's kind of hard to have family in your church name and be down on mothers holding babies in church.

At Mission Community Church in Gilbert, Arizona, I witnessed the most amazing mom on the front row of an evening service. She had her baby on her lap and did the following without taking her eyes off of the pulpit:

1. Bounced her baby on her right knee

2. Opened the diaper bag on her left knee

3. Pulled out an empty baby bottle

4. Pulled out a container of formula

5. Took the cap off of a full bottle of water and poured it into the baby bottle

6. Poured two scoops of formula into the baby bottle

7. Shook the baby bottle to mix the formula

8. Fed her baby

She never skipped a beat bouncing that baby. I was amazed and thought to myself, *I've got to get done with this sermon before she changes that baby's diaper!* It never ceases to surprise me when I see a mom balancing craziness while providing tender care. This is one more way that children uniquely bear the image of God to the world.

Parents provide for children. They provide protection and life's necessities. Parents of past generations rested at night knowing that they had provided the basics: food, clothing, and shelter. Today's parents are stressed to provide way beyond the basics. We feel as though we need to provide every opportunity and advantage: big moments on the stage and playing field and big scores on standardized tests. This is not the provision that the Scripture talks about. In Matthew, Jesus gives us one of the Bible's clearest teachings on dual image-bearing between parents and children:

> "Which of you, if your son asks for bread, will give him a stone? Or if he asks for a fish, will give him a snake? If you, then, though you are evil, know how to give good gifts to your children, how much more will your Father in heaven give good gifts to those who ask him!" (Matthew 7:9–11)

Even though parents are sinful, they have an innate desire to provide for their children. However, their best attempts to provide and care for their child pale in comparison to the way our heavenly Father loves and provides for us. Every time a parent provides for a child it's a reminder of this great truth.

Parents are placed in a child's life to prioritize Jesus as the main relationship.

Jesus is the most important relationship in a child's life, not Mom and Dad. Parents are placed in a child's life to prioritize Jesus as the main relationship.

A few years ago, I baptized my daughter at Dogwood Canyon outside of Branson, Missouri. When she came up out of the water I whispered in her ear, "Jesus is your priority relationship, not me." It was a very emotional defining moment.

The next year at the Branson RecPlex, I baptized my son, Carson. As he came up out of the water, I whispered the same thing in his ear, "Jesus is your priority relationship, not me." I barely got the statement out of my mouth when Carson stuck his finger in my face and said, "You better not cry." He was too late.

First John 3:1 says: "See what great love the Father has lavished on us, that we should be called children of God! And that is what we are!" We are the children of God and dependent on Him for protection and provision. We come to Him as children. We depend on God, and our children are a daily reminder of that. As they need us, so we need the Father.

EMPOWERING EVERYONE IN THE HOME

Singles: The next time you head home for the holidays or a special event, prepare an honor list for each of your parents. Read it out loud in front of family and friends. Watch what honor does to build your close-knit family.

Spouses: One of the greatest gifts you give your children is showing honor to your spouse. Speak words of high value over your spouse and let your children know that you appreciate and value Dad or Mom.

Parents: Remind your children of your desire for Jesus to be the priority relationship. Children leave home. Until that day, we prepare them to be responsible adults who love Jesus. The days go slow, but the years go fast. How we value the time says much about how we value our children.

FAMILY CONVERSATION STARTERS

1. Tell your children about the day of their birth.
2. What do children teach us about the kingdom of heaven?
3. Is Jesus the priority relationship in our home, or do we place other relationships before Him?
4. What are some ways our culture devalues children?
5. What can our family do to value the children of our community and the world?

CHAPTER 4

ANSWERING QUESTIONS

WHAT TO SAY WHEN YOUR CHILDREN
ASK ABOUT YOUR FAITH

*"Children have been loaned to us temporarily for the
purpose of loving them and instilling a foundation of
values on which their future lives will be built."*

—JAMES DOBSON

M y friend Dan Seaborn says, "At some point every teenager
loses his or her brain. Parents need to pray and be patient
until the brain one day returns." It may happen in their twenties or
thirties. Some of you are praying for a brain to come back into your
forty-year-old. Keep praying and believing.

Fortunately for us, the Internet was not around when we were
kids. There's no record of the times our brains fell out. Kids today
capture moments on their mobile devices, and many bad moments
get uploaded and remain online forever.

My brother, Andy, is grateful technology was not around when he decided to take me mudding in his new non-four-wheel-drive truck. The fact that his truck did not have four-wheel drive is an important detail in this mudding story.

At age sixteen, Andy got his license and a used Ford F-100. I was thirteen years old and thankful to have another driver in the family. One of my first rides in his truck was a late night trip home from our church youth group. We lived two miles from the church, but on this night it might as well have been twenty-two miles. With corn fields on both sides of the road, our rural drive was tempting for the owner of a truck.

About halfway home, Andy turned to me and asked, "You wanna go muddin'?"

Muddin' wasn't really in my blood. I was the editor and photographer of my junior-high yearbook and a benchwarmer on our basketball team. Risk taking and living life on the edge didn't flow through me. Driving into a corn field to do donuts didn't sound like fun to me, but I was the passenger and had little to say in the decision.

About a mile from home he pulled into a freshly plowed field and punched it. This is a good time to remind you that this was a two-wheel-drive truck. You know what happened? In the middle of the field, we bogged down.

"Get out and push," Andy insisted. I think my eye roll expressed my level of enthusiasm.

A thirteen-year-old pushing an F-100 out of a corn field has never been done in the history of mankind, but we were going to try. After a few minutes, he yelled out the truck, "Try rocking it." I wiped the mud out of my eyes and honored his request.

All our efforts got us more stuck, so we abandoned the truck and jogged home.

One the way home we worked on our story. There are a few important items children need to know about making up a story: First, make sure the two parties to the conspiracy have the same story. Parents are expert interrogators and they love pointing out inconsistencies. Second, make sure the evidence supports the story. In our case, it didn't.

It was late by the time we got home, and our parents were in bed. Andy woke them up and told them the story while I waited at the bottom of the stairs.

Andy convincingly said, "I lost my wallet. I think it fell down on the floor board so we pulled off the side of the road, and I started looking for it and I couldn't find it. Then we got stuck."

He walked out of the bedroom and looked at me with thumbs up as if to say, "We've got this."

I reminded him, "They're buying the story right now because they think your truck is on the side of the road, but when they pull up and see it a half mile out in a cornfield, we'll be dead meat."

Andy responded, "I thought about that. We're going to tell them we got stuck on the edge, and we just had to start rocking it." "And we rocked it a half mile out?" I exclaimed under my breath . . . not to mention that Dad will see that we rocked your truck in circles a half mile out.

Late that night, Mom and Dad graciously asked a few questions as they dressed, then we all piled in the car. On the mile drive back to the crime scene, I thought, "Dad is calm now. He's being a good dad and helping his kids out of a bind. But he's going to flip his lid when he sees the truck in the middle of a corn field surrounded by donut evidence."

> *Parents understand astonishment. Children say and do things that leave us speechless.*

I looked over at my brother and couldn't believe he thought this story would stick. What is it about teenagers that makes them think Mom and Dad are ignorant? The moment a child thinks Mom and Dad are gullible is when their brains fall out.

As we approached the scene, I counted down to Dad's explosion. He would feel astonished.

"Andy, would you like to revise your story? Would you like to tell me what really happened?" he asked.

Andy stuck with the wallet story. This is called "digging yourself a deeper hole." Dad had just extended some grace, and we blew it. Dad had an astonished look while mom remained silent. She was astonished, too.

"Son, what were you thinking? Why would you take your two-wheel-drive truck into the middle of the corn field?" He continued prodding.

Andy eventually came clean, and a local farmer towed the truck for us.

The word *astonished* combines the emotions of frustration and confusion. Both are primary emotions that lead to anger. Being frustrated with a situation and confused with what the child was thinking brings on the situation.

The apostle Paul uses the word *astonished* to describe his confusion and frustration when new believers abandoned their faith in Jesus for legalism: "I am astonished that you are so quickly deserting the one who called you to live in the grace of Christ and are turning to a different gospel—which is really no gospel at all. Evidently some people are throwing you into confusion and are trying to pervert the gospel of Christ" (Galatians 1:6–7). Paul's astonishment was justified. He had led them to Jesus, plus nothing minus nothing, and now false teachers were telling them that they weren't truly Christians. Paul was confused and frustrated in his attempts to bring them back to pure and simple faith in Jesus.

Parents understand astonishment. Children say and do things that leave us speechless. We often think and sometimes say, "What were you thinking?" This is why God gives children parents. Parents help children find their brains. When children start asking questions, parents are the first to give answers. Parents help children process God and life.

CHILDREN AND QUESTIONS

Do you remember bringing your first child home from the hospital? Were you surprised the hospital staff let you do it? I was. I remember them wheeling in the television cart with instructional videos. There is something on your chart in the hospital that tells them you're a first-time parent. The videos informed me that I was clueless when it came to caring for a child.

You think about all the animals and plants that have not fared well in your home and now they are giving you a human to care for. What? After you install the car seat in the hospital parking lot for the first time, you realize, "This child's story has begun. It's time to go home."

As children grow, they ask thousands of questions. You and I will answer hundreds of thousands of questions in a child's lifetime. My kids ask so many questions, I started categorizing them.

There are bribery questions. "Who's the best dad in the world?" This is usually met with a follow-up question from the parent, "What do you want?"

There are boredom questions. "How much longer until we get there?" My grandma Mary Jane started every road trip by giving each grandson a roll of nickels. Every time you asked a question about distance, time, or the destination, you had to give her a nickel. With inflation, you'd probably need quarters today.

Often our day will start with, "What are we doing today?" At the beginning of the day they want to make plans to avoid boredom at all costs.

There are impossible hypothetical questions. These have no answers, at least no right answers. My friend Charles Billingsly's son, Cooper, is the best at these questions. Charles started writing them down and now has a collection over 600 questions. Here are some he texted to me:

"If it were 2,331 degrees outside for a quarter of a second, would we die?"
"Would you rather be distracted for your whole life or nervous?"
"If you could be a picture, where would you want to hang?"
"Mom, can you ground Dad?"
"In Bible times, what did they use to moisturize their lips?"

"Can you imagine how good a volcano must feel after it erupts?"

"Dad, did they ever have sunny days in The Dark Ages?"[10]

There are connection questions. "Whatcha doin'?" These questions are typically asked in passing but often lead to special moments. All you must do is take the time to slow down and engage. This is an important category because it sets the parent up for what I consider the most important category.

The faith and purpose questions are the most important questions. As children grow, their questions get more serious and weighty. "Where do babies come from?" "Why are we here?" "What is my purpose?" "Is my life significant?" "Do I fit in?" "Is there a place for me in the world?"

Parents establish their child's worldview by answering questions.

Charles Swindoll is known for saying, "Family is where life makes up its mind." Family is where you get questions answered for the very first time. Family is where you and I begin to process life. Answering questions is a primary role of a parent and sets the course for a child's life. Parents establish their child's worldview by answering questions.

Denise Bevins, our ministry director at Woodland Hills Family Church, is the servant of all. She is the most solid, steady, Jesus-loving wife, mom, and grandmother I know.

I walked into her office on a Tuesday morning in April 2014 stressed about the week's message. As I shared with her about the role of parents answering questions in the lives of their children,

I said, "Tell me about your parents and how they answered life's questions for you." Her eyes immediately filled with tears. She told me her story in a way I had never heard it before. She shared in great detail. I asked her if she would be willing to share with the congregation, and she agreed. She asked if she could write it out, and I would read it. Here is what she shared that Sunday:

My parents divorced when I was nine years old. My father struggled with alcohol, and when he started getting physically abusive with my mother, she left him. After the divorce, I saw him twice. Being the oldest of six kids and watching my mother struggle to support us, I grew very resentful towards my father. Not only was he not there physically and emotionally, but he didn't provide any financial support. My mother was raised a practicing Catholic, in a practicing Catholic home. She would send us to church, but since she was divorced, she never felt the church would accept her. She was faithful in having us pray for our meals, occasionally talking about God, but nothing about Jesus.

As a teenager, I lived a wild and defiant lifestyle, and I made many bad choices. Somehow, I graduated from high school. I was in a low-income family, and the state of California provided opportunities for low-income youth to have summer jobs. They offered me a job working at the Highway Patrol office and that's where I met my husband, Don. Actually, I met him when my speeding caught his attention while driving in his territory on Highway 101, two days before starting my new job at the California State Highway Patrol.

Don was raised in a strong Christian home. His father loved Jesus and walked with Him his entire life. He loved his wife wholeheartedly for sixty-five years. He was very proud of her accomplishment of becoming a teacher, and although he never graduated from high school, he humbly built a successful business selling mobile homes and was known for excellent customer service.

My father-in-law was loved by everyone who knew him. Although he could preach a great sermon, generally his witness was in how he lived. His character was spotless. Every fruit of the Spirit was in him, and his spiritual gift was generosity. I would best describe him as the closest human likeness of Jesus I have ever known.

I can't remember any fuss when Don and I told them we were getting married. At that time, I had no interest in hearing the gospel. My heart was hardened, but I desired to feel accepted and loved, and my father-in-law was gifted in that area. He loved me as his own and the words "I love you" were spoken often. He was great at asking questions about things I was interested in. It was important to him that he knew me.

My heart softened, and I asked Jesus into my heart three years into my marriage. Looking back now, I can see God's love and care for me. He knew exactly what it would take for me to know that I could trust His unconditional love by placing this man in my life. I had the honor of calling him my dad.

Denise had a father-in-law who loved her and engaged with her questions. His questions in return showed his love and care. He took the time to hear her. Sometimes just fielding the question is more important than having an immediate answer.

Parents don't always have the answers, but that's okay. Why? Because we can get the answer someplace. When I was in seminary, I had a first-year professor who worked a week ahead of his students. The professors who had been teaching for thirty years were never caught off-guard. They heard every question and had scripted answers. This was not true with the first-year professors. They needed time to get the answers. When someone asked that first-year professor a question that he couldn't answer, he would simply say, "I'll have an answer for you the next time we meet." I think a great answer parents can have ready for the truly baffling questions is, "I don't know, but I'll find out for you."

QUESTIONS LINK FAITH AND FAMILY

Questions give parents the opportunity to link faith and family. Deuteronomy 6 gives us the clearest teaching on this. We get the what, how, and why in the clearest outline, and it's all summed up in a simple question.

What

These are the commands, decrees and laws the LORD your God directed me to teach you to observe in the land that you are crossing the Jordan to possess, so that you, your children and their children after them may fear the LORD your God as long as you live by keeping all his decrees and commands that I give you, and so that you may enjoy long life. Hear, Israel, and be careful to obey so that it may go well with you and that you may increase greatly in a land flowing with milk and honey, just as the LORD, the God of your ancestors, promised you.

Questions give parents the opportunity to link faith and family.

Hear, O Israel: The LORD our God, the LORD is one. Love the LORD your God with all your heart and with all your soul and with all your strength.

How

These commandments that I give you today are to be on your hearts. Impress them on your children. Talk about them when you sit at home and when you walk along the road, when you lie down and when you get up. Tie them as symbols on your hands and bind them on your foreheads. Write them on the doorframes of your houses and on your gates.

When the LORD your God brings you into the land he swore to your fathers, to Abraham, Isaac and Jacob, to give you—a land with large, flourishing cities you did not build, houses filled with all kinds of good things you did not provide, wells you did not dig, and vineyards and olive groves you did not plant—then when you eat and are satisfied, be careful that you do not forget the LORD, who brought you out of Egypt, out of the land of slavery.

Fear the LORD your God, serve him only and take your oaths in his name. Do not follow other gods, the gods of the peoples around you; for the LORD your God, who is among you, is a jealous God and his anger will burn against you, and he will destroy you from the face of the land. Do not put the LORD your God to the test as you did at Massah. Be sure to keep the commands of the LORD your God and the stipulations and decrees he has given you. Do what is right and good in the LORD's sight, so that it may go well with you and you may go in and take over the good land the LORD promised on oath to your ancestors, thrusting out all your enemies before you, as the LORD said.

Why (Watch how the question ties it all together.)

In the future, *when your son asks you,* "What is the meaning of the stipulations, decrees and laws the LORD our God has commanded you?" tell him: "We were slaves of Pharaoh in Egypt, but the LORD brought us out of Egypt with a mighty hand. Before our eyes the LORD sent signs and wonders—great and terrible—on Egypt and Pharaoh and his whole household. But he brought us out from there to bring us in and give us the land he promised on oath to our ancestors. The LORD commanded us to obey all these decrees and to fear the LORD our God, so that we might always prosper and be kept alive, as is the case today. And if we are careful to obey all this law before the LORD our God, as he has commanded us, that will be our righteousness" (Deuteronomy 6:1–25, italics mine).

In verses 1–5, to paraphrase Moses, he was saying, "Listen, these aren't my words, these are the words of your Father. The words I'm sharing with you right now are directed to you. I'm the one sharing it, but it's coming to you from the LORD God." The phrase "The LORD" is used twenty-five times so we don't forget where the words originated.

After they possessed the land of Israel, it was open before them and all they had to do was settle it. What did "settle it" mean? It meant driving out the Canaanites. This wasn't an imperialistic take over. It had nothing to do with economics or racism. God wanted the Canaanites along with their idols to be gone from the land. He didn't want His children to be surrounded by the idols and pagan religions. He wanted them to serve the only true God; He wanted them to serve Him.

There are four truths in verse 4: (1) There is a God; (2) there is only one God; (3) He is the Lord; (4) and He is our Lord. God wants our full devotion and worship.

Verses 6–19 give a clear strategy for centering our lives around the Lord. When you wake up, until you go to bed, and all through the day, talk about the Lord. Make Him the center of your daily conversation. *Tell your children why you believe what you believe.* When enjoying a meal at home, talk about Him. At work, share Him. On your journey, discuss Him. Write His name everywhere so you'll remember Him.

God directed His people to enjoy the land, cities, houses, furnishings, wells, vineyards, wine, olive groves, and meals He provided for them. He wanted them to receive these things with thanksgiving. But He didn't want them to get caught up in the way the pagans lived. He wanted them to do everything in His name and to follow Him as their ancestors had. They were to prioritize faithfulness.

In verses 20–25, we get to the question. "Dad, what is the meaning of all of this?" "Why do we do this?" "Why do we serve the

Lord?" "Why do we follow Him?" "Why do we love Him?" "Why do we obey the Lord?"

When your children ask these questions, give them the great story of salvation. Give them the gospel. Tell your children why you believe what you believe.

I once heard the story of young mom who cut the ends off of her ham and placed it in the pan for cooking. One day her daughter asked, "Mom, why do you cut off the ends of the ham before you put it in the pan and into the oven?"

"I don't know, but let me ask your grandma," the mom answered.

So she called her mom and asked, "Mom, why do you cut the ends off the ham before you place it in the pan and into the oven?"

"I don't know, but let me ask your grandma," the mom answered.

So grandma called her mom and asked, "Mom, why do you cut the ends off the ham before you place it in the pan and into the oven?"

"I have a small pan," great grandma replied.

Going through the motions of prayer, church attendance, tithing, and Bible reading is not enough. At some point, our kids ask, "Why do we do all of this?" Knowing the answer to that question is critically important in connecting your child to a personal faith in Jesus. "Because I said so" and "This is what we have always done" are two bad answers to that question.

How will your children learn of salvation and God's grace from you?

I refuse to grow old and grumpy. When I'm asked the weighty and at times difficult-to-answer questions of faith, I want to be patient, humble, and transparent in my answers. Fortunately, I get to lean on others to help me answer these questions.

HELP YOUR CHILDREN NOT TO FORGET

In Deuteronomy 6, the Lord implored His children not to forget Him when they entered the land and began to enjoy all that He had provided for them. The book of Judges continues the story for us. Watch what happened after God's children entered the land:

> After Joshua had dismissed the Israelites, they went to take possession of the land, each to their own inheritance. The people served the LORD throughout the lifetime of Joshua and of the elders who outlived him and who had seen all the great things the LORD had done for Israel.
>
> Joshua son of Nun, the servant of the LORD, died at the age of a hundred and ten. And they buried him in the land of his inheritance, at Timnath Heres in the hill country of Ephraim, north of Mount Gaash.
>
> After that whole generation had been gathered to their ancestors, another generation grew up who knew neither the LORD nor what he had done for Israel. Then the Israelites did evil in the eyes of the LORD and served the Baals. They forsook the LORD, the God of their ancestors, who had brought them out of Egypt. They followed and worshiped various gods of the peoples around them. They aroused the LORD to anger because they forsook him and served Baal and the Ashtoreths. In his anger against Israel the LORD gave them into the hands of raiders who plundered them. He sold them in to the hands of their enemies all around, whom they

were no longer able to resist. Whenever Israel went out to fight, the hand of the LORD was against them to defeat them, just as he had sworn to them. They were in great distress.

Then the Lord raised up judges, who saved them out of the hands of these raiders. Yet they would not listen to their judges but prostituted themselves to other gods and worshiped them. They quickly turned from the way of their ancestors, who had been obedient to the LORD's commands. Whenever the LORD raised up a judge for them, he was with the judge and saved them out of the hands of their enemies as long as the judge lived; for the LORD relented because of their groaning under those who oppressed and afflicted them. But when the judge died, the people returned to ways even more corrupt than those of their ancestors, following other gods and serving and worshiping them. They refused to give up their evil practices and stubborn ways.

Therefore the LORD was very angry with Israel and said, "Because this nation has violated the covenant I ordained for their ancestors and has not listened to me, I will no longer drive out before them any of the nations Joshua left when he died. I will use them to test Israel and see whether they will keep the way of the LORD and walk in it as their ancestors did." The LORD had allowed those nations to remain; he did not drive them out at once by giving them into the hands of Joshua. (Judges 2:6–23)

Joshua was God's chosen successor for Moses. He brought the people into the land. His generation served the Lord, but the next generation did not. Can we relate to that today? They knew about God's mighty power displayed in the exodus from Egypt. However, they didn't hold to the truths about God and make them personal.

When we forget what our parents taught us, God will send others along to remind us.

This is why Deuteronomy 6 was written. It was written to help God's people avoid forgetting Him. However, God's grace is relentless. In the midst of their unfaithfulness, He continued to save them. In the midst of their pursuit of foreign gods, God continued to reach out to them.

I think most parents can relate to anger and love at the same time. We ask our kids, "What were you thinking?" Often, we ask it in a frustrated tone. At the same time, no matter how bad our kids mess up and sin, we still love them and want to rescue them.

The same is true with God. When the people forgot, God raised up judges to remind them. This is a great truth for parents with adult children who have strayed from God's truths. This is great encouragement for parents with prodigals.

I've sat with parents and heard their painful story of a prodigal. The stories of withdrawal from the family, drug and alcohol addiction, cohabitation, prison, and even reckless death, are all too common in families today. In the midst of mourning, parents say, "We tried our best. We did everything we knew to do. Why did this happen? Why did he turn his back on God?"

This is one reason for these great Old Testament stories. They remind us of when God's children turned their backs on Him. No matter how badly they rebelled and how long God tarried, He never gave up on them. He pursued them relentlessly.

When we forget what our parents taught us, God will send others along to remind us. At our church, everything we do is committed to the parent-child relationship. We partner with parents to be an additional voice in their child's life, including an additional voice for the adult child.

Parents already know how to create environments because we do it when our children are small. We pick schools, churches, friends, activities, and neighborhoods to set our children up for success. We create environments to bring good influence around our kids. We know that academics and athletics don't raise adults, parents do.

Providing Additional Voices of Influence

One way parents provide additional voices is to create environments for the adult child to experience other voices of influence. There are a few ways to do this.

Invite your adult child to special weekends at church. If your child is far from God, leverage Easter, Christmas, Mother's Day, and Father's Day. Let them know that you don't need gifts or a fancy lunch. All you want is for them to sit next to you during the message.

More than once I've heard a parent say, "Ted, you shared something this morning that I have been sharing for years." It's amazing how hearing the same thing from someone else has a tendency to sink in.

Invite your adult child to serve with you at church.

Maybe your son or daughter regularly attends church but they are timid to join or volunteer in a ministry. Invite them to join in what you are doing.

I love what God is doing in the Gumm and Harrell family at our church. Matt Gumm is our worship leader and his wife, Katie, makes sure the technical details come together each Sunday morning.

Katie's dad is R. P. Harrell, one of the best musical directors and pianists in the country. R. P. puts on a rough tough exterior, but he's the biggest softy on the planet. I've enjoyed becoming friends with him because of what God is doing in his family.

Recently an entertainer in our town lost his son suddenly. Who was the first person he called? He called R. P. This has happened multiple times over the years in our town and R. P. usually ends up calling me with the news.

When R. P. told me about this young man's death I said, "R. P., have you noticed that when tragedy strikes a family in this town, you're the first person they call?" It's not the church office. It's you. Do you know why they call you? It's because they say to themselves, 'If God can change this guy's heart, he can change me.' They are watching that in you."

What does it mean to create an environment of serving for your family? R. P. plays the keyboard at our church, whether he likes it or not. I say that in jest, but it's sort of true. He loves Matt and Katie. He started attending Woodland Hills because of Matt and Katie. He serves because of Matt and Katie. Now they serve together. This is a beautiful picture of God at work in a family and using additional voices of influence.

Invite your child over for dinner with other folks from church.

Where do conversations begin with other voices of influence? It starts around kitchen tables and in living rooms. If there is no way your child will attend church, consider this thought from Max Lucado:

> "Long before the church had pulpits and baptisteries, she had kitchens and dinner tables. 'The believers met together in the Temple every day. They ate together in their homes, happy to share their food with joyful hearts' (Acts 2:46). Hospitality and hospital come from the same Latin word meaning healing. Sharing your family's table sends the message that, 'You matter to me and to God.'"[11]

Use your home to influence your child. Use the influence of others to remind him or her of what you believe. Be intentional with meals around your family table. Invite additional voices to share a meal with your entire family.

Find ways to offer grace to your adult children relentlessly even though they don't seek it or appreciate it.

Remember Denise Bevins from the beginning of this chapter and the love, acceptance, and influence of her father-in-law? Well, Denise knows how to create environments for her children to be surrounded by other voices of influence. She runs our volunteer and welcome ministry at church.

Her son, Cedric, gives golf-cart rides from the parking lot to the worship center for our guests and members. He loves it, and it shows.

Her daughter, Savonnah, serves the children in Critter Street. She is faithful, and we are grateful.

Her husband, Don, is part of our security team. He keeps us safe and takes his job very seriously. Don't mess with him.

Her grandchildren serve our church each week as well. No one in Denise's family simply attends church; they serve the church as a family. I've watched God work in her family through serving.

Mom and Dad, don't give up on your adult children. Get creative. Find ways to offer grace to your adult children relentlessly even though they don't seek it or appreciate it. No matter what they've done, no matter what they've said, no matter how hard they've gone against you, no matter how much they've rejected you, no matter how many times they remind you that they can't stand what you taught them, offer them grace, because that's what your heavenly Father does for you.

EMPOWERING EVERYONE IN THE HOME

Singles: Unanswered questions from childhood can find answers in biblical community. Plug into the local church. Join a small group or Bible study. Invite a trusted, wise leader to coffee and dialogue over life's weighty questions.

Spouses: As a united front in the home, you can lean on each other to answer questions. If you disagree about the answer, offer grace to one another and allow the children to see a healthy discussion as your work through differences.

Parents: You don't need all the answers, but you do need to know where to go to find them. The best response to a difficult question is often, "I don't know, but I'll get back to you on this."

FAMILY CONVERSATION STARTERS

1. Discuss the events of the day of each child's birth.
2. Describe your hometown. (If you live close, plan a field trip.)
3. How did you feel bringing each child home from the hospital?
4. How is the culture around you shaping your home?
5. What questions has the world answered for us? What does God's Word say in response?

6. What is the best part of coming home each night?

7. What did you hear today that negatively impacts your family and your story?

CHAPTER 5

WORKING HARD

FAMILIES THAT EARN, GIVE, AND SAVE MORE THAN THEY SPEND

*"You have to teach children about money intentionally—
create teachable moments."*

—DAVE RAMSEY

I was eleven years old when my dad and I had our first, big fight. It sparked a month-long debate over whether a child should pay taxes. With attitude I said, "Dad, no way does the government expect a child to pay taxes."

Dad calmly responded with, "You made good money this year and received a 1099 in the mail. That means you must file a tax return. This is going to be a great lesson to prepare you for life in the real world." My dad loves the expression "real world." At sixty-six, he's still saying, "Welcome to the real world."

I contacted a tax attorney to verify my dad's claims. I tried to prove my dad wrong, but I failed. That year I owed around $1,500.00

to the IRS. My dad took me to the bank to withdraw the money from my bank account. How dare he? It's humorous to think that was the same year I became interested in politics. I don't know what was harder to take, paying the taxes or my dad's enthusiasm that I paid taxes.

I dedicate this chapter to my father, Ron Cunningham. He taught me that the character and work ethic necessary to provide for a family is the same character and work ethic required to form healthy relationships within the family.

The formula is simple: *work hard, give much, save enough, and consume less.* I believe this formula brings your life and family under control and fuels a thriving home.

When I was growing up, our family attended church Sunday morning, Sunday night, and Wednesday night. Every time the doors were open, we were there. My parents loved the Lord and were committed to raising their sons in a Bible-believing church. If you do the math, before I left home at age twenty-two I had listened to over 3,400 sermons. That number doesn't include Sunday school lessons, revivals, conferences, or convocations at Liberty University.

After listening to thousands of sermons in my youth, I can't remember the titles or outlines. However, I do remember the lessons. They stuck with me. A sermon reinforces what is being taught and lived out at home. Children listen and watch their parents and more than likely repeat the behavior and lessons they hear and observe.

My mom and dad encouraged me to work hard at a very early age. They taught me to "Go to the ant, you sluggard; consider its ways and be wise" (Proverbs 6:6). The type of work a person does is part of competency, but hard work flows from character.

Hard work means that you're willing to do any job while you wait for the "perfect" job to come along. Don't let your kids grow up to be like cousin Eddie from the movie *Christmas Vacation*, who refused to work because he was holding out for a management position. Cousin Eddie had the maturity of a little boy. Little boys make bad husbands and fathers.

Before I turned twenty-two, my resume included:

Landscaping (mowed lawns in the neighborhood)
Busboy (corner restaurant in Naperville, Illinois)
Caddy (Naperville Country Club)
Handyman (Valley Baptist Church, Oswego, Illinois)
Groundskeeper (Oswego School District #308)
Print shop worker (Chattanooga, Tennessee)
Store clerk (Lion Photo at the Fox Valley Mall)
Photographer (freelance)
Academic computing (Liberty University)
Snow shoveling (Christmas break in Naperville, Illinois)

As early as I can remember, my parents told my brother and me, "We're going to provide you with three things: food, clothing, and shelter. That's our responsibility as parents. Gifts come on holidays and birthdays. If you want extras, you need to earn them. You need to get out there and work."

They didn't start this off right away. They waited until I was about six before they made me earn. At six years old, I had a wallet with cash. If a neighbor's yard needed mowing, Dad sent me to do it.

My mom and dad never put out the expectation that they would pay 100 percent of my college expenses. They had the money, but they wanted me to earn a college education. Some people might think they were mean for withholding the funds, but now at forty years old, I'm grateful to them. They sent me off to college and said, "You're going to have to work. I know you might want to do classes during the day and then shoot hoops in afternoon, but that's only if you have time after work and studies." They valued productivity. Thank you, Mom and Dad!

FIRST, TEACH YOUR CHILDREN TO EARN

At a recent conference, a mom with preschoolers came up to me and said, "Before we go to bed every night, we listen to Dave Ramsey as a family." Some people read children's devotional Bibles, but this family does Financial Peace University. I love it! She told me that her preschoolers are huge Dave Ramsey fans.

She said, "You can ask my four-year-old this question: 'Where do you go when you want money?' and she screams out enthusiastically, 'You go to work!'" That's so great!

I've met folks who love their jobs, but I've never met anyone with the perfect job.

It's a mindset that doesn't expect others to give you money. You go out and earn it even when you don't feel like it. That's the antidote to entitlement.

I've met folks who love their jobs, but I've never met anyone with the perfect job. We live in a fallen world and perfection is unattainable. That said, I heard recently of someone in my family who had the near-perfect job. It was my great-grandfather, William Ludwig.

Heading north on I-55 from St. Louis to Chicago, look off to your left as you cross Exit 90. The farmland surrounding that exit was owned by my great-grandfather. When the contractors started building the overpass, they approached him and asked if they could use the dirt from his land. If he agreed, they would build him a pond and stock it with fish.

Midwesterners see this often: one or two small farm ponds near the overpasses. That's where the dirt comes from to build the overpasses. I love fishing those small ponds. Anytime you can contain the fish, well let's just say that's a good day on the water.

So, the state of Illinois built my great-grandfather a pond. They paid him $2,000 a day for the entire summer it took to build the pond. I picture great-grandpa sitting in his lawn chair near the site watching the trucks pull in and out. What a job!

That summer job came with an incredible bonus. They returned every year to stock the pond for him. What? You've got to be kidding! This even continued after his death. When he passed away, my Aunt Dorothy and Uncle Dick took over the property, and every year a truck full of fish showed up to bless them.

There are many farmers in my family who worked hard to make a living. I must guard my heart from entitlement, the desire to have in three years what my great-grandpa spent a lifetime accumulating.

While I waited for the "perfect" job to come along, I had some really bad ones. The worst job I ever had was with my brother, the hardest worker I've ever met in my life. I remember roofing a house with him when I was fifteen years old. Andy was in charge of the job, and I was his laborer. If you ever get the opportunity to be a laborer for your older brother, don't do it.

My first task was to deliver bundles of shingles up a ladder and onto the roof. This was exhausting and time-consuming. Imagine my anger and frustration years later when I drove by a construction site and saw a conveyor belt delivering shingles up to the roof. I called and asked my brother, "Andy, where was that when I needed it?"

He said, "Yeah, that's what we paid you to do."

On your hardest most grueling days at work, you must remind yourself that work has always been part of God's plan. Work is not the result of sin. Before the fall in Genesis 3, we read in chapter 2, "The LORD God took the man and put him in the Garden of Eden to work it and take care of it" (verse 15). Burdensome work was not part of creation. Before the fall, work was enjoyable and rewarding. Sin brought judgment and with it grueling, difficult work.

Do you ever look around and appreciate all the different ways to make a living? This is a discipline I added to my routine recently. Workers are everywhere. Take time to appreciate the waiter or the waitress in the restaurant. See the value in the person who delivers your mail or picks up the trash. Value the guy who fixes your HVAC when it breaks down. Hard work provides for family.

Historically and biblically, the primary motivator to work is hunger. We work hard to put food on the table. Empty stomachs motivate us:

> "There is a way that appears to be right, but in the end it leads to death.
> The appetite of laborers works for them; their hunger drives them on." (Proverbs 16:25–26)

Tonight would be a good time to begin discussing work as a family. This is the purpose for the family conversation starters at the end of each chapter. Start by talking about hard jobs you've had. Discuss the different ways a person earns money. One of the

What we teach our children about work translates into relationships.

reasons we value the conversation around the family table about the grind of life and hard work is so that our kids understand that food doesn't magically appear. It takes work. This teaching builds the responsibility necessary for your children to care for their own families one day.

What we teach our children about work translates into relationships. Teach them that you don't need to leave a job just because it gets hard. For the same reason, you don't leave a marriage or family because it gets hard. Your marriage and family will experience struggle and difficulty over a lifetime. True character stays the course and gets the job done no matter the circumstance. Taking charge of hard work means you take personal responsibility for difficult seasons in relationships.

Proverbs 12:11 says, "Those who work their land will have abundant food, but those who chase fantasies have no sense." Have you ever met anyone who chases fantasies? It's the person who is in a new job every three, four, or five months because the job didn't make millions immediately, or the boss offended them, or the hours were too demanding. Success typically doesn't come overnight. It's built step by step. Just like compatibility in marriage, it doesn't just happen. You build it over time.

One of the reasons businesses fail when they are handed down from parents to children is because the children haven't developed the work ethic to maintain what was built by the hard work of their parents. Like winning the lottery, many who come into millions instantly aren't prepared for it. They end up in a mess because they don't have the money skills to handle the windfall.

So how do we get our kids working at an early age without breaking the law? I love that my eleven-year-old daughter is begging us for a job right now. I'm not going to deter her enthusiasm one bit. Instead, we'll discuss her skills and competencies. Discovering and developing work skills can start at any age.

The following list is part of our premarital counseling at Woodland Hills Family Church. How a young couple provides for their new marriage is important to us. This list is also a great guide for parents to help identify skills in elementary-aged kids, tweens, and teens. Spend some time around the family table discussing the following skills:

Entertaining: to perform, act, dance, speak, or do magic (this tops the list when you live in a town like Branson, Missouri)

Artistic: to conceptualize, picture, draw, paint, photograph, or make renderings

Graphics: to lay out, design, and create visual displays or banners

Planning: to strategize, design, and organize programs and events

Managing: to supervise people to accomplish a task and coordinate the details involved

Counseling: to listen, encourage, and guide with sensitivity

Teaching: to explain, train, demonstrate, or tutor

Writing: to write articles, letters, or books

Repairing: to fix, restore, or maintain

Feeding: to create meals for large or small groups of people

Mechanical: to operate equipment, tools, or machinery

Counting: to work with numbers, data, or money

Serving: to wait tables, make beds, or clean rooms

Public relations: to handle complaints and customers with care and courtesy

Welcoming: to convey warmth, develop rapport, and make others feel comfortable

Landscaping: to mow, weed-eat, garden, and work with plants

Decorating: to beautify a setting for a special event

Maintenance: to efficiently maintain something that is already organized[12]

After you assess skills, draw some lines between skills and actual jobs. Take a look at the following eighteen jobs and discuss some ways to earn money at an early age:

1. Housesitting—feed fish, water plants, walk animals

2. Yard work—mow lawns, pull weeds, remove debris

3. Seasonal work—shovel snow, rake leaves, plant flowers

4. Garage sales—gather items, mark prices, work tables

5. Car wash—wash, dry, vacuum

6. Housework—wash windows, dust baseboards, power-wash decks and driveways

7. Construction assistant—set up equipment, clean worksite, handle supplies

8. Attractions/theaters—sell tickets, usher, theme park attendant, mini-golf/go-kart attendant

9. Retail sales—cashier, greeter, shelf stocker

10. Veterinary office—groomer, kennel attendant, vet assistant

11. Hospitality—receptionist, housekeeper

12. Construction—plumbing, electrical, concrete, roofing, carpentry

13. Information systems—manage websites, PC maintenance, create apps

14. Restaurant—wait tables, bus tables, cook, host/hostess

15. Marina—pump gas, rent boats, give lessons

16. Pool—lifeguard, concessions, maintenance

17. Golf course—mow, pick the range, work in the pro shop

18. Farm—feed animals, clean stalls, work the fields

I'm grateful for parents and other adults in my life who allowed me to pursue work at an early age. There were times I thought they conspired against me. Like the time my pastor hired the junior high boys to dig ditches for the new building project. We knew a Ditch Witch would knock that job out in a couple of days, but he preferred to employ us over a couple of weeks. Today I'm grateful.

Even if your job is extremely difficult and stressful, know that Jesus is your ultimate boss.

I learned that the ability to earn money is a gift from God at my church. Ecclesiastes 5 explains it this way: "This is what I have observed to be good: that it is appropriate for a person to eat, to drink and to find satisfaction in their toilsome labor under the sun during the few days of life God has given them—for this is their lot. Moreover, when God gives someone wealth and possessions and the ability to enjoy them, to accept their lot and be happy in their toil—this is a gift of God. They seldom reflect on the days of their life, because God keeps them occupied with gladness of heart" (vv. 18–20).

Appreciate the work God gives you. As you drive to work this week, thank Him for the ability to earn. Even if your job is extremely difficult and stressful, know that Jesus is your ultimate boss. Colossians 3:23–24 says, "Whatever you do, work at it with all your heart, as working for the Lord, not for human masters, since you know that you will receive an inheritance from the Lord as a reward. It is the Lord Christ you are serving." Your ultimate boss is not the HR manager, CEO, or department head. He or she may cut your check, but your work is a testimony to the Lord.

This perspective turns every job into a ministry. Jesus is the one you report to. Punching in late isn't an issue with your boss; it's an issue between you and Jesus. Turning a twenty-minute break into forty minutes is an issue before the Lord. Work is discipleship, and it reveals our true character.

What would happen if our children spent as much time thinking about earning as they did spending? A couple of changes would be seen immediately.

First, children who earn have a proper value on money. Have you ever been in a store and your child asks how much something costs? You respond by saying, "$50.00," and they respond with, "That's not bad." Really? They are eight years old and think fifty bucks is not much money? If your son or daughter spends a week or two earning fifty bucks, they won't be as quick to let it go.

I heard from one dad in Florida after his family livestreamed a message on earning at our church. Immediately following the message, his kids went to a family friend's pear tree and gathered fruit. They went door-to-door selling them and made a profit of $48.00. Fantastic! I can't begin to tell you what that does to my heart as a dad and a pastor. What children learn about the value of earning money and providing for themselves will help them their entire lives.

One day my son was hanging with his friends and talking about dogs. His friend Ty said, "We really want to get a dog, but we're kind of low on money right now."

Overhearing the conversation, I said, "Ty, we are all low on money right now, but there are plenty of ways to earn it." He nodded in agreement.

Second, children who earn are more thankful. My therapist friend, Ryan Pannell, defines prolonged adolescence as too much privilege and not enough responsibility. At its root, entitlement grows. The best definition of entitlement I've heard comes from another pastor friend, Carey Nieuwhof: "Entitlement is thinking you have a right to something that is a privilege."

I highly recommend Carey's leadership podcast. He understands how prolonged adolescence impacts the workplace, and he equips leaders with skills to eradicate entitlement. Carey invited me on his podcast this past summer and shared with me two thoughts that are gold. First, when you give your kids something they should have worked for, it replaces incentive with entitlement. I want to bless my kids with every advantage, but what happens when giving our children every advantage becomes a disadvantage? There are some things they can work for and when we don't have them work for it, entitlement sets in. Second, kids who feel entitled to everything will be grateful for nothing. Kids who feel entitled to nothing will be grateful for everything. If I ever find that on a plaque at a Christian bookstore, I'm going to buy it.

Kids who feel entitled to everything will be grateful for nothing. Kids who feel entitled to nothing will be grateful for everything.

SECOND, TEACH YOUR CHILDREN TO GIVE

Gary Smalley is one of the most grateful and generous individuals I know. The more I watch his life, the more I see how gratefulness and generosity tie together. He has been my mentor for thirteen years. On more than one occasion I have witnessed his generosity. His two favorite ways to bless people makes for a reality show I have yet to see.

He loves to buy people groceries. When he gets to the checkout and places his items on the conveyor belt, he removes the plastic divider between his groceries and the items of the person in front of him. I've seen the exchange more than once. He moves it off the conveyor belt and the other person puts it back. After a brief awkward moment, Gary says, "I've gone all day without doing something nice for someone, if you wouldn't mind I'd like to buy your groceries." You can't imagine the number of people who have resisted this act of kindness. I've witnessed the resistance, but I've also witnessed the tears and hugs. Generosity is contagious.

Gary also loves to buy tires. Once at Walmart he noticed the couple in line ahead of him struggling to make a decision between two tires and four. Gary stepped up and said, "Would you mind if I buy you four tires?" You know how Oprah has a reputation for generosity because of the car giveaway? I feel the same way when I get around people like Gary. When he refreshes others, it refreshes me. If you ever see Gary at Walmart or the grocery store, make sure you follow him to the checkout. I'm joking (a little).

Give With a Cheerful Heart

When you earn money, the first question you should ask is, "What am I going to give?" not "What am I going to spend?" Proverbs 3:9 says, "Honor the LORD with your wealth, with the firstfruits of all your crops." This proverb comes out of Deuteronomy 26:1–11:

> When you have entered the land the LORD your God is giving you as an inheritance and have taken possession

of it and settled in it, take some of the firstfruits of all that you produce from the soil of the land the LORD your God is giving you and put them in a basket. Then go to the place the LORD your God will choose as a dwelling for his Name and say to the priest in office at the time, "I declare today to the LORD your God that I have come to the land the LORD swore to our ancestors to give us." The priest shall take the basket from your hands and set it down in front of the altar of the LORD your God. Then you shall declare before the LORD your God: "My father was a wandering Aramean, and he went down into Egypt with a few people and lived there and became a great nation, powerful and numerous. But the Egyptians mistreated us and made us suffer, subjecting us to harsh labor. Then we cried out to the LORD, the God of our ancestors, and the LORD heard our voice and saw our misery, toil and oppression. So the Lord brought us out of Egypt with a mighty hand and an outstretched arm, with great terror and with signs and wonders. He brought us to this place and gave us this land, a land flowing with milk and honey; and now I bring the firstfruits of the soil that you, LORD, have given me." Place the basket before the LORD your God and bow down before him. Then you and the Levites and the foreigners residing among you shall rejoice in all the good things the LORD your God has given to you and your household.

God delivered the children of Israel from bondage in Egypt. He brought them into a land flowing with milk and honey. They responded by taking the firstfruits of the soil and bringing them in a basket to the Levites. It was a sacrifice, an understanding of true ownership. God owns everything. When we tithe, we recognize His ownership.

This is the foundation for firstfruits giving. With a mighty hand and an outstretched arm, we have salvation, we've been rescued, and we've been redeemed. In Jesus, we live and move and have our being. He gives us breath each day. He enables us to work. We enjoy what He brings to us, and when we tithe, we give back to Him. Giving recognizes Jesus as the Giver of all life.

In the 1965 movie *Shenandoah,* the farmer, played by Jimmy Stewart, offers a dinner prayer with an attitude that confuses and misplaces the whole idea of ownership. If you get a chance, look up this twenty-two-second clip on Youtube:

Lord, we cleared this land. We plowed it, sowed, and harvested it. We cooked the harvest. It wouldn't be here, we wouldn't be eating it if we hadn't done it all ourselves. We worked dog bone hard for every crumb and morsel, but we thank you just the same anyway, Lord, for this food we're about to eat. Amen.

A few years ago, I preached at Mission Community Church in Phoenix, Arizona. When they announced that it was time to take an offering, the congregation erupted in cheers. We've been cheering at Woodland Hills in Branson, Missouri, ever since. When we rejoice in giving, God is pleased.

The apostle Paul put it this way in 2 Corinthians 9: "Remember this: Whoever sows sparingly will also reap sparingly, and whoever sows generously will also reap generously. Each of you should give what you have decided in your heart to give, not reluctantly or under compulsion, for God loves a cheerful giver" (vv. 6–7). We want to be excited about giving. We want to know that what we are doing matters and that we are able to bless others as a result of it.

Giving recognizes Jesus as the Giver of all life.

Give to Refresh Others

Proverbs 11:24–25 says, "One person gives freely, yet gains even more; another withholds unduly, but comes to poverty. A generous person will prosper; whoever refreshes others will be refreshed."

Giving is an adrenaline rush! It blesses the giver every bit as much, if not more, than the recipient. I found this to be true with my wife's dad and grandpa.

Denny and Lloyd shared a passion for metal detecting. I didn't grow up in a metal detecting family, but Amy did. My first exposure to this hobby was in the late 1990s in Fremont, Nebraska. I planned on a laid back day, but had no idea what was coming.

We pulled up to the high school grounds on a Saturday morning. No one was around. Denny headed for the sports field. Lloyd headed for the bleachers. Never have I seen two grown men so excited over finding pennies, nickels, and dimes. Every time one made a discovery, the other one heard about it. Then they celebrated together. After an hour or so we headed for home.

A couple of days later, we went out again and this time, I decided to take a pocketful of change. I wanted this to be the best day of their lives.

When we arrived at the new location, I decided to tag along with grandpa Lloyd. He was eighty years old and a jolly man. I followed a few feet behind him and threw a few coins at a time over his shoulder. He found every coin I threw. At one point he screamed over to Denny, "Get over here! It's just laying on top of the ground." Denny raced over and now I had to keep two guys busy. They laughed, bounced around, and had a ball. So did I.

When they were done, they got in the front seat of the car and I got in the back. As they counted their three to four dollars, Denny asked his dad, "Have you ever had a day like this?"

"No, never!" Lloyd said with exasperation.

I faced a moral dilemma. Should I tell them? I asked my congregation this question once and about 2 percent in attendance that morning said, "Yes." I must assume those were our guests.

To this day, my father-in-law remembers that outing. So do I. Just the mention of it sparks laughter in us.

A Secret Key to Great Relationships

Giving without expectation of anything coming back to you is at the heart of ministry. I saw this years ago on a Sunday morning at a church in Lancaster, Pennsylvania.

On the front row, I worshiped alongside a sweet eighty-year-old African-American woman. She swayed with the music, and her heart overflowed with love for the Lord. I'm a more conservative worshiper, which means my hands rarely come above my shoulders. She was the opposite. Her hands spent little time below her shoulders.

About three songs in, she decided it was time to participate with me. She started tapping me on the shoulder and arm with perfect timing to the beat of the music. I winced at first, but then got used to it. She almost turned my slight swaying into an all-out charismatic morning. All I can say is, she was precious.

Right before the preaching, the pastor stood up to take an offering. As he shared the needs and ministries of the church, she reached for her purse and pulled out her offering envelope. She then leaned over to me, showed me the envelope and said, "Look at this?"

Giving without expectation of anything coming back to you is at the heart of ministry.

It wasn't the amount that brought a smile to my face, for it was a meager sum. It was the way she had decorated the envelope that was equally as precious as she was. Every square inch of that envelope had either a sticker, drawing, or verse written across it. She poured her heart into preparing her offering.

That scene has stuck with me for years. I typically write a tithe check on my way out the door on Sunday morning. To be perfectly honest with you, I sometimes don't give it much thought. It's automatic and often lacks a worshipful, joyful expression.

Giving, just like earning, is a spiritual issue that flows from the heart. I don't want it to become routine. I want it to be an overflow of my life. Our family wants our giving to be generous, cheerful, and thoughtful.

Families struggle with codependency because behavior in the home is transactional. We give, love, and serve expecting something in return. You give to your spouse with a truckload of expectation. You pour in to your kids expecting them to make you look good. When you give, serve, and love with expectation, it always leads to manipulation. On the flip side, giving, serving, and loving without expectation leads to meaningful ministry and healthy families.

THIRD, TEACH YOUR CHILDREN TO SAVE

Proverbs 21:20 says, "The wise store up choice food and olive oil, but fools gulp theirs down." The fool never thinks ahead. The wise person plans for emergencies, lean earning years, and caring for family and parents when they can't care for themselves.

Dave Ramsey encourages people to have an emergency fund of $1,000.00. At times that number seems low to me, but it's doable for every family. Margin is the space between your load and limit. Financial margin is making sure you have some space between your expenses and income. This margin is necessary for every family because the future is uncertain and life is short.

Every family, regardless of income, can make little deposits into a savings account over long periods of time. Wise, prudent savers don't count on a day when they will stumble into millions of dollars. Instead, they consistently put away some of the little amounts they earn. Anyone can start saving at any time.

Years ago I heard someone say, "The problem with the American Dream is people are stressed with what they'll do with a million dollars they'll never have." I don't plan to win the lottery because I don't play the lottery. Our plan is to work hard, give much, live on less than we make, and save for years down the road.

Proverbs 13:11 says, "Dishonest money dwindles away, but whoever gathers money little by little makes it grow." We don't live for get-rich-quick schemes, nor do we plan on fast savings plans. Patience is the key to saving.

The question isn't "Should we save?" The big question is "How much should we save for later down the road or retirement?" I don't claim to be a money expert, so I rely on the counsel of others. Proverbs 15:22 says, "Plans fail for lack of counsel, but with many advisers they succeed." At the top of my list of advisers in this area are Michael Hyatt and Dave Ramsey.

Until recently, my thoughts about retirement were guided by the investment commercials on television. You've seen them, right? They can be

> *Anyone can start saving at any time.*

quite stressful. Do I need half a million or three million to live out my senior years? Most of them tap into an inner voice that says, "You'll be broke when you're old!" Scary!

I'm not alone with these feelings. In the summer of 2014 I went on Facebook and asked our congregation to fill in the blank on this statement: "Retirement is _____."

Here are just a few of the 100-plus responses I received:

Jennifer said, "Something other people, somehow, seem to be saving for!"
Kim said, "Unlikely!!!!"
Heather said, "Not in my future."
Susan said, "A word made up for rich people, I will have to work until my body stops letting me."
Sandy said, "Something I'll never get to experience."

Melinda said, "Gonna take a miracle."

Bill said, "Never going to happen to me."

Carl said, "Never going to happen."

Bev said, "In my dreams."

Dillion said, "Not going to happen in my lifetime."

Michael Hyatt opened my eyes to whole new way of thinking about retirement. His take on the golden years brought a paradigm shift to our family. In a blogpost called "Why Retirement Is a Dirty Word," he said:

> The more I think about the purpose and meaning of work, the more I'm convinced that nothing destroys our sense of purpose and health more than the modern notion of retirement. It's detrimental to us individually and collectively.
>
> The idea is that you can induce someone to do repetitive, soul-killing work with little emotional benefit if you promise a big enough carrot at the end of the stick. For people in my parents' generation, it was the only way to keep the machine rolling.
>
> This is a terrible and dehumanizing way to think of work. It assumes that workers have no real value beyond output.
>
> The only way to get workers to play along is to convince them that the pasture is lush and relaxing. Suck it up now because it's going to be wonderful in a few decades.[13]

God calls us to find satisfaction in our work. Whatever you do, work for the Lord. Find great meaning in where He has you right now, not where you will be twenty or thirty years down the road. Don't wish away this season of life. Embrace it. Enjoy it. Be grateful for it.

Save for the future without hoarding. Hope in God, not your savings account. Years ago I heard one pastor say, "I hope God doesn't bring us out of the recession too quickly. There's a lot more we need to learn." Did you catch that? God has much to teach us about wealth and wealth-building. I think the first, most important lesson is don't misplace your trust in it.

Paul put it this way to young Timothy, "Command those who are rich in this present world not to be arrogant nor to put their hope in wealth, which is so uncertain, but to put their hope in God, who richly provides us with everything for our enjoyment" (1 Timothy 6:17).

Jesus said,

"Can any one of you by worrying add a single hour to your life? And why do you worry about clothes? See how the flowers of the field grow. They do not labor or spin. Yet I tell you that not even Solomon in all his splendor was dressed like one of these. If that is how God clothes the grass of the field, which is here today and tomorrow is thrown into the fire, will he not much more clothe you—you of little faith? So do not worry, saying, 'What shall we eat?' or 'What shall we drink?' or 'What shall we wear?' For the pagans run after all these things, and your heavenly Father knows that you need them." (Matthew 6:27–32)

FOURTH, TEACH YOUR CHILDREN
HOW TO SPEND WISELY

We're all consumers. We need to eat. Our children must be clothed. All of us rest our heads somewhere each night. We spend money every day. The real issue is not whether we spend money, but how we spend money. Your family's spending motives flow from the heart and determine your spending habits.

Of the following spending habits, which one or two best describes your family?

1. Ego Spending.
This is focusing on yourself while being indifferent to the needs of others. This doesn't even have to be outside your family or your community. Part of the joy of being the spiritual leader in the home is that we get to take the extra and give it to the others in our family rather than spending it on technology and toys for ourselves. There's nothing wrong with technology and toys, but is your spending focused on you more than those in your family?

2. Entitled Spending.
This confuses privilege for necessity by feeling you deserve or need something. My generation wants in three years what our parents spent thirty years accumulating. Air, clothes, food, water, and shelter fall into the need category. The latest phone, computer, and specialty coffee drinks are most definitely privileges.

3. Emotional Spending.
This is making purchases to medicate pain, hurt, or loss. It's closely related to emotional eating. Soothing your emotions with

spending is short-lived. Stay out of the malls and offline when you are feeling down.

4. Envy Spending.

You want what somebody else has. "Why shouldn't I have that if they have it?" "Why shouldn't I get it because they got it, and we're kind of in the same status, right? We're in the same season of life."

> *The real issue is not whether we spend money, but how we spend money.*

5. Essential Spending.

This type of spending gets by with the basics. This would define my parents' and grandparents' generation. This is why my parents order only water in restaurants. They save thousands a year with this motive. We don't need the best of everything, we don't need to spend a ton; we can get by with the basics.

6. Extravagant Spending.

People caught in this spending habit choose the top-of-the-line best in every category. This is the opposite of essential spending.

7. Exhausted Spending.

This happens when excessive spending fatigues you. It usually happens around the holidays or vacations. You have no energy left because you have no money left.

Solomon said,

Whoever loves money never has enough; whoever loves wealth is never satisfied with their income. This too is meaningless.

As goods increase, so do those who consume them. And what benefit are they to the owners except to feast their eyes on them? (Ecclesiastes 5:10–11)

We're consumed with consuming. We can't get enough. Studies are now conducted to answer the question, "When is enough, enough?"

One well-publicized study last year put the optimal income for happiness at around $75,000. Rising income, it turns out, produces greater happiness until you get to around $75,000. After that, there are diminishing returns, with more income leading to little or no gain.

The latest to weigh in on the issue is Skandia International's Wealth Sentiment Monitor. It found that the global average "happiness income" is around $161,000 for 13 countries surveyed. The United States wasn't specifically measured.

But there was a wide range of answers depending on the country. Dubai residents need the most to feel wealthy. They said they needed $276,150 to be happy. Singapore came in second place, with $227,553, followed by Hong Kong, with $197,702.

Germans only need $85,781

The French need $114,000

The British need $133,000.

Surveys show that among Americans, most say they need $1 million or more to feel wealthy.

How much wealth or income would you need to feel happy?[14]

"Spend less, enjoy more" is our family motto. Find more joy at home rather than at the mall. Don't feel the pressure to give your children everything they ask for. Avoid debt, and its stress. Remember, "The rich rule over the poor, and the borrower is slave to the lender" (Proverbs 22:7).

Your family may need to get as drastic as my pastor friend in Canada did when he went on a spending fast. He spent no money on "extras" for an entire year. It was tough, but he says it completely changed his priorities. You may consider a one-week or one-month family spending fast just to see where your want-o-meter is at. It may be the solution to changing the demands for stuff in the home. Eradicate the kid-centered home, which produces self-centered children. When there is money left in the budget, explain to them why they don't get it. Prioritize a date with your spouse when there are a few extra bucks at the end of the week. If the kids whine or complain, tell them to start a lemonade stand.

Abigail Van Buren said, "If you want your children to turn out well, spend twice as much time with them and half as much money."

Pastor Eugene Cho says, "Generosity is what keeps the things we own from owning us." I love it. Everything comes back to generosity.

Solomon said,

Everyone comes naked from their mother's womb, and as everyone comes, so they depart. They take nothing from their toil that they can carry in their hands. (Ecclesiastes 5:15)

What do you say?

EMPOWERING EVERYONE IN THE HOME

Singles: Before marriage, work hard and keep your spending under control. One of the best ways to prepare for marriage is to eliminate debt. Pay off school loans and live on a budget. This will allow you to start your marriage with a financial margin.

Spouses: Take control of your family's finances. Agree on a plan before introducing it to the entire family. Show your children how you sacrifice for each other.

Parents: Get serious about the responsibility of work in the home. Eradicate prolonged adolescence by giving your children jobs to do around the house. Some jobs don't come with a paycheck because it's just part of being in the family. Find extra jobs where they can earn a little extra spending money. Consider an allowance and walk them through how much to give, save, and spend. Envelopes are great teaching tools to help with this.

FAMILY CONVERSATION STARTERS

1. Write the words *earn, give, save,* and *spend* on four pieces of paper. Ask your kids to arrange them in the proper order. Discuss why they chose the order they did. (Correct order: earn, give, save, and spend.)

2. Consider these questions to help you think about the importance of earning a living:

   • Where do we go when we want money?

- What would be the perfect job?

- Describe the worst job.

3. Since Jesus is your ultimate boss, read the following
    verse then discuss some ways to turn a job into
    a ministry: "Whatever you do, work at it with all
    your heart, as working for the Lord, not for human
    masters, since you know that you will receive an
    inheritance from the Lord as a reward. It is the Lord
    Christ you are serving" (Colossians 3:23–24).

4. Mom and Dad, share some of the jobs you have
    worked in your lifetime.

5. After we earn money, what should be our first
    response? "What should we get?" or "What should
    we give?"

6. List a few activities or expenses you can cut out of
    your family budget in order to give more.

7. If you make $10 mowing a yard or babysitting,
    what do you think the "earn, give, save, and spend"
    breakdown should be?

    _____ tithe

    _____ missions

    _____ savings

    _____ spending

8. What are some of your long term goals for saving?

9. The Christian investor hopes in God, not wealth.
    How do we balance our need to save with our trust

in God? How can we best guard our hearts from hoarding and greed?

10. Start a grateful list as a family. Gratefulness is an antidote to selfishness, entitlement, and greed. List five things you are grateful for.

11. What are some ways you can guard your hearts from greed, ungratefulness, and the love of money?

12. How would a budget help your family control spending and be content? What would you add to your budget? What would you remove from your budget?

13. If your family were to go on a spending fast for one week, what should you not spend money on?

14. What's the difference between a want and a need?

CHAPTER 6

FORMING RELATIONSHIPS

WHY CHARACTER TRUMPS
COMPATIBILITY AND CHEMISTRY

*"Friendship is a deep oneness that develops when
two people, speaking the truth in love to one
another, journey together to the same horizon."*

—TIMOTHY KELLER

In the spring of 2014, our family purchased a chicken coop. It came in a box with some assembly required. It should have read, "Much assembly required." My daughter and I gathered the tools early one Saturday morning and started on the home for our chicks that were growing larger each day.

As we assembled the coop I sang the Farmersonly.com online dating commercial to my daughter: *You don't have to be lonely at farmersonly.com. City folks just don't get it.*

"Corynn, you *are* going to marry a farmer, aren't you?" I asked.

With her cowboy boots on, she said, "I don't know Dad, it's way too early for that."

"I know, but I just want you to know that I'd be great with you marrying a cowboy and living on a farm or a ranch," I noted, "After all, you are passionate about animals."

For the entire hour it took us to assemble that coop, we talked about relationship formation. The message is simple and important but often left out of family conversations.

I said, "Corynn, I'm not that concerned with the type of work your husband pursues. The bigger issue is how hard he works." Since I've never met a lazy farmer, I wanted Corynn to prioritize character, and the work ethic that flows from it, in what she finds attractive in a man. With that said, we introduced our chicks to their new home.

Online dating is on the rise. There's absolutely nothing wrong with meeting someone online so long as you follow the decision-making milestones of traditional relationship formation. Oh yeah, and you should also have a good online profile and name.

A recent Google search of online dating profiles found the following bad names:

1. MyMomLuvsMe

2. AdorableSleeper24

3. MySeptumIsPierced35

4. UnemployedButLooking29

The following list is better than the first list but still cracks me up:

1. ManlyBeardMan

2. Love2Hunt

3. Love2Fish

4. PapaSmurf72

Whatever name you go with, never forget, a good match is a good start but it won't sustain a thriving marriage. Only character does that. Great marriages prioritize character over compatibility. Spend your dating time inspecting character more than similarities and differences. Early in relationship formation we like to focus on similarities and downplay differences. To do so neglects the weightier issue. Spend more time looking deep into how the person you date handles differences than you do figuring out what differences you have.

Amy and I built our home seven years ago around a gigantic, one-hundred-year-old oak tree. It was a beautiful tree. The problem was I didn't inspect the tree before we built our house. It turns out the tree was completely hollow. In bed at night, we heard branches falling on the roof. The tree was dying and falling down around us. I brought a tree inspector out and he said, "Don't let the kids play around this tree or they will surely die." It was a beautiful, perfectly shaped tree on the outside, but hollow and dying on the inside. This also happens in relationship formation. You fall for an attractive exterior, only to find later that the person is hollow on the inside.

A good match is a good start, but compatibility is developed over a long time. Compatibility is not something you test for, stumble into, or discover. You create it with character. Compatibility is forged in the muck and mire of conflict.

> *Compatibility requires skills you develop and implement over a lifetime. The more you practice these skills, the better you get.*

Compatibility requires skills you develop and implement over a lifetime. The more you practice these skills, the better you get. This is why you should be more compatible after twenty years of marriage than after five years of marriage. You have fifteen more years of advanced skills training.

As one pastor said recently, "Don't use the term *soul mates* until you've been married at least thirty years." I agree. You *become* soul mates, you don't find one online.

One of my favorite stories about compatibility is from a couple of my dear friends, Jon and Heather Jenkins. As newlyweds, they vacationed in the Northwest. Jon loves fly fishing, and they spent several days on their trip fishing together.

On one of those days, their marriage was tested. Jon describes the scenery. Heather describes the situation. It was a beautiful stream that meandered through the landscape. He said it felt a little like a ditch because the sides came straight down to the creek. To get in the creek, you had to slide down the bank. The conditions of that day were perfect for fishing.

They worked their way down the stream enjoying life and fishing together. At one particular bend in the creek, they turned the corner and came face-to-face with a moose. You really don't know someone until you're standing shoulder to shoulder with them, staring at a moose. They say the moose seemed happy until he started snorting. With moss hanging from his rack, he let Jon and Heather know, "This is my creek." Their adventure suddenly became a life-threatening situation.

I have to pause the story right there to let you know there are two endings to this story. Jon and Heather each have a version. I think it's only fair that you know both.

Heather says, "We feared for our lives!" Jon turned to the bank, elbowed her out of the way and climbed to safety, leaving her to face certain death . . . alone.

To this day, Jon insists that he was getting to the top of the bank first so he could help Heather out. We weren't there, so we'll never know. Heather still insists, "His enthusiasm to get out of that creek didn't feel to me like he was trying to save my life."

You don't really know a person until you face a snorting moose together. Think about that for just a second. You can date, you can chat online, but you don't know a person's character until you are in a car with them, stuck on a highway in traffic for an hour and a half, and late for a flight. That's when you learn who the person truly is.

I enjoy premarital counseling. My favorite session is when a young-and-in-love couple sits down and I ask them, "Tell me about your last fight." The purpose of this question is to help them with the skills necessary to resolve conflict.

On more than one occasion, I've heard, "Pastor, that's the amazing thing. We don't fight."

"Okay, well what might cause potential conflict in your marriage?" I ask.

They look at each other, giggle, then say, "Well we've talked about that, and we don't see any potential conflict."

Do you know what they need? They need a moose.

They need a traffic jam.

They need a bill they can't pay.

They need a mortgage on a home.

They need children.

This is why character is so important. Taking charge of relationships flows from your character. When you take charge of your faith and family, you don't react or blame what is going on around you. You make healthy decisions together as a couple no matter the dire circumstances you find yourself in.

Duke University ethics professor Stanley Hauerwas says, "The primary challenge of marriage is learning how to love and care for the stranger to whom you find yourself married."[15] I couldn't agree more.

> *Never allow the mundaneness of life to trump curiosity and fascination in your marriage.*

Your marriage will go through many different seasons. We have no idea how we will respond or react to a situation ten years from now. We have no control over the situation, but we do have control over our response. Character chooses the right response no matter what. Amy and I choose to love and enjoy life together, even when hard times hit us. Staying happily married is a choice each spouse must make. Take charge of your choice. When your spouse goes through different seasons, find new ways to love and care for him or her. Never stop discovering your mate. Never allow the mundaneness of life to trump curiosity and fascination in your marriage. Live in awe of the "stranger to whom you find yourself married."

According to a recent article in *Psychology Today,* "Compatibility does not hinge on some personal inventory of traits. Compatibility isn't something you have. It's something you make. It's a process, one that you negotiate as you go along. Again and again. It's a disposition, an attitude, a willingness to work."[16]

Taking charge of a relationship means making the daily decision to work, fight, love, reconcile, pray, and enjoy life together.

We hate to use the words *negotiate* and *compromise* when it comes to love. However, that's the truest of loves. I love my wife, and one of the best ways I show her that love is to make personal decisions with her in mind. I want her to know I'm not independently deciding while neglecting her thoughts, opinions, or feelings. Compatibility says, "I want to get to know you and make decisions with both of us in mind." Any other way is simply selfishness.

That article continues with this thought, "Chemistry is an alluring concept, but much too frequently people use it to absolve themselves of the need to consciously examine their approach to one another. It keeps you from opening your own heart, embracing an unwavering willingness to do the hard work of exploring, knowing and respecting the other person."[17] Taking charge of relationship formation begins and ends with respect for the other person. When a relationship deteriorates, it's because one or both spouses move away from the process of compatibility into self-preservation mode.

We have a socially acceptable statement we make today when we want out of a relationship or marriage: "We're not compatible." What that really means is, "We choose to no longer get along." Taking charge of a relationship means making the daily decision to work, fight, love, reconcile, pray, and enjoy life together.

Compatibility is a choice and a process. We choose to work out our differences, live in curiosity and fascination, and persevere through hard times. This works out over time through listening, understanding, and validating each other in frequent conversation. Discovery says, "I want to get to know you."

The reason television commercials for online dating highlight compatibility as the key to great relationships is because we have spent so much time learning to be independent. We value independence as citizens, employees, and even church members. "This is who I am, and I need to find someone who accepts me for who I am. I need someone who will not make me change who I am." So we look for jobs, communities, churches, and spouses who accept us more than we try to adapt to or change for them. This is the fundamental problem with modern notions of compatibility and chemistry.

Pastor Timothy Keller at Redeemer Church in New York City notes this tension when he says, "The reason that marriage is so painful and yet wonderful is because it is a reflection of the gospel, which is painful and wonderful at once. The gospel is this: We are more sinful and flawed in ourselves than we ever dared believe, yet at the very same time we are more loved and accepted in Jesus Christ than we ever dared hope."[18]

In relationships, we like to focus on the "loved and accepted" part of the equation and avoid the "sinful and flawed" part. When compatibility is all about acceptance for who you are, you rob yourself of the refining process. Becoming compatible means we each take personal responsibility for our sinfulness. I never expect my spouse to take charge of or accept my sin. My interaction with Amy often reveals my sin, but she is in no way responsible for it. Marriage is a daily picture of the gospel in my home. This is why marriage as normative and singleness as the exception is part of our relationship formation teaching at Woodland Hills Family Church.

A few years back when we started our Twoignite Sundays at church, many singles expressed concern for the regular marriage teaching in a church with so many singles. Again, I validate this concern. One of our single members, Janae Bass, sent me an email recently that validated both her struggle with and our desire to regularly teach on marriage:

> I just wanted to tell you thank you. Your message last spring on godly character completely changed my perspective on dating. Last year at this exact time I was really struggling with singleness. Coming to church on Twoignite Sundays was incredibly painful for me. Four years of hearing marriage sermons was taking a toll on this single girl. It literally felt like I was an alcoholic coming to church in a bar. I knew God would come through, but I was in a place of doubt. I started praying that God would change my heart, as I could feel it growing more and more bitter. And slowly He did. Right about that time Clayton reentered my life. I was excited at the potential, but also terrified of being hurt.

I was putting walls up around my walls and setting expectations no man could reach.

The night before your message on godly character I remember sitting in my room telling Hope Bronn I wasn't sure about Clayton because I always thought I would marry a pastor. She said, "No way! You can't marry a pastor, you're the ministry one! You need a rock who can support your craziness!" She's pretty wise for a seventeen-year-old. Then the next morning you said it doesn't matter what a person does. You said, "I don't care what profession Corynn's husband is in, as long as he has Godly character."

It all clicked for me in that moment. God opened my eyes to the gift He had placed in front of me. I write all of this to thank you. Thank you for sticking with marriage ministry and prioritizing it at Woodland Hills. Even if I didn't always appreciate it, I do now! I actually can't wait for church on Sunday!

—Thank you, Janae

According to Focus on the Family's *The Family Project*, "Humanity's first and most fundamental problem was isolation. God solved this problem by joining Adam and Eve in a relationship to fully reflect His image in the world."

Humanity's first fundamental problem was isolation, not sin. God created Adam and placed him in Eden to work. Genesis 2:15 says, "The LORD God took the man and put him in the Garden of Eden to work it and take care of it." Adam was a zoologist. He named the animals. My daughter thinks this job is awesome.

However, God's purpose for man is not limited to work. He created Adam to be with another:

The LORD God said, "It is not good for the man to be alone. I will make a helper suitable for him."

Now the LORD God had formed out of the ground all the wild animals and all the birds in the sky. He brought them to the man to see what he would name them; and whatever the man called each living creature, that was its name. So the man gave names to all the livestock, the birds in the sky and all the wild animals.

But for Adam no suitable helper was found. So the LORD God caused the man to fall into a deep sleep; and while he was sleeping, he took one of the man's ribs and then closed up the place with flesh. Then the LORD God made a woman from the rib he had taken out of the man, and he brought her to the man.

The man said,

"This is now bone of my bones and flesh of my flesh; she shall be called 'woman,' for she was taken out of man." That is why a man leaves his father and mother and is united to his wife, and they become one flesh. (Genesis 2:18–24)

I like to joke with my wife and give a paraphrased commentary on this text when I say, "Part of God's plan in creation included man taking a nap." The Lord called it a "deep sleep." It's biblical.

Here is how Genesis 2:18–24 breaks down. Adam started with, "Okay, that's a cow, that's an antelope, that's a bison." If he had been in the Ozarks and driving down the road, he would've said "That's a possum, that's a vulture, that's a vulture eating a possum." He named the animals up through verse 20.

Pastor Matt Chandler from the Village Church in Dallas, Texas, points out that something significant happens in verse 23. When Adam saw Eve for the first time, the tone in his voice changed. He didn't add her to the list of new animal names. Instead, he began to sing. It went something like this: "There's a cow, there's a dog, there's a cat, there's a vulture, there's a raven, there's a crow, there's an eagle. There is Wooooomaaann!"

That's a great question to ask men. Do you have a song in your heart when you see your wife? In the midst of work and the daily grind, does something light up in you when she walks into the room? It did early in your dating, engagement, and marriage. Music stirs us. Marriage stirs us, too.

One Sunday in September 2014, I asked the men of Woodland Hills Family Church a musical question. Hundreds of hands shot up when I asked, "Does anyone out there have a couple song?" The follow-up to that question didn't have nearly as many hands: "Any men in here willing to sing that song if I hand you a microphone?" I grabbed the mic and headed into the congregation.

Hoping no one would sing, "You ain't nothing but a hound dog," I handed the mic to the first guy, and he belted out, "I, I'm so in love with you, Whatever you want to do is all right with me, 'cause you make me feel so brand new, and I want to spend my life with you," by Al Green. The congregation went nuts. The second guy I handed the mic to sang a few lines of "Always and Forever." Again, it was met with overwhelming cheers. In another service, a husband sang, "God Bless the Broken Road" by Rascal Flatts. Each guy sang it directly to his wife. It was a special morning that we are still talking about.

I have two songs for Amy. The first is "Amy, what you gonna do. I think I could stay with you for a while maybe longer if I do." The other is, "Brown eyed girl. Sha la la la la la la la la la la dee dah."

SEASONAL GIFTS OF GRACE

Proverbs 18:22 says, "He who finds a wife finds what is good and receives favor from the LORD." We believe, according to the Scripture, that marriage is normative and should be promoted. Both singleness and marriage are seasonal gifts of grace.

> *Both singleness and marriage are seasonal gifts of grace.*

In 1 Corinthians 7:7, Paul refers to both singleness and marriage as a gift: "I wish that all of you were as I am. But each of you has your own gift from God; one has this gift, another has that." Pastor Vaughan Roberts clearly describes the nature of these gifts:

> When Paul speaks of singleness as a gift, he isn't speaking of a particular ability some people have to be contentedly single. Rather, he's speaking of the state of being single. As long as you have it, it's a gift from God, just as marriage will be God's gift if you ever receive it. We should receive our situation in life, whether it is singleness or marriage, as a gift of God's grace to us.[19]

First Corinthians 7:7 is one of the most misquoted, misunderstood verses of this chapter. It's important to note that there are many different singles in many different seasons of life. It behooves us to spend some time thinking through the different ways people experience and use their season of singleness. Here are six singles we minister to in the church today:

Single and Content.

This is using singleness to serve the Lord. This person is not rushing marriage, but they're not opposed to the possibility either.

This Christ-centered contentedness is not to be confused with selfishness. I challenge the unnecessary delay of marriage to those who seek a prolonged vacation from the responsibility of work and relationship. My advice is don't rush marriage, but don't avoid it either.

Single and Impatient.

Young women in the church ask, "Where are the men?" I usually say, "Be patient with your church as we continue to challenge the young men to step up and pursue responsibility." I believe many are hearing the message and eradicating their prolonged adolescence by taking charge of their faith and lives. We must not confuse patience and idleness. Anticipation of marriage is healthy. The cliché joke on college campuses goes something like, "Ring by spring." While you wait, prepare yourself to be a fantastic spouse. Redeem the time and be productive.

Divorced and Dating.

To those recently divorced and now dating, you need time to heal and to seek biblical counseling and restoration for your soul. Don't date to medicate the heartache. You might be thinking, "That's easy for you to say, but I haven't had someone show me love and affection in quite some time. It feels good, and I feel like I deserve it after the nightmare marriage I just came out of." I hear you, and that's why you need to give God time to heal you. Another person can't do that. For the sake of your future and those around you, don't rush into a new relationship.

Divorced and Remaining Single.

There are many reasons to remain single after divorce. Jesus addresses the primary reason in Matthew 19:9: "I tell you that anyone who divorces his wife, except for sexual immorality, and marries another woman commits adultery." You must honestly assess the "why" behind divorce. Was it a trivial reason? Was it persistent, relentless, unrepentant adultery? There are many important questions to answer that affect your walk with Christ. Remain single until you can answer those questions with integrity, and seek wise counsel in this process.

Widowed.

The church is called to give special attention and care to this group of singles: "Religion that God our Father accepts as pure and faultless is this: to look after orphans and widows in their distress and to keep oneself from being polluted by the world" (James 1:27). My grandma was a widow for over thirty years. With the love and support of her three daughters, three son-in-laws, and six grandsons, she was well taken care of. My mom and her sisters modeled 1 Timothy 5:3-4 for us: "Give proper recognition to those widows who are really in need. But if a widow has children or grandchildren, these should learn first of all to put their religion into practice by caring for their own family and so repaying their parents and grandparents, for this is pleasing to God." Care for the widows in your family, for this pleases God.

Married and Alone.

Though technically and legally married, some spouses are functionally single. They feel like the butler or the maid. There is no intimacy in their marriage. Communication is gone. Finances and children have kept the spouses together, but each feels all alone. I encourage these spouses to start today to turn their marriage around. It starts with each person. Each spouse can choose to make necessary changes, regardless of the actions of the other person in the marriage.

My friend Bob Paul is a vice president at Focus on the Family and leads their National Institute of Marriage. He told me years ago that it only takes one spouse to begin turning a marriage around. Rest in Jesus as your source of life and companion in your loneliness. Begin serving and loving your spouse with the love that only Jesus gives. He came to serve, not to be served. Pray that God will soften the heart of your spouse. The best marriage on the planet exists when both spouses connect to the true and only Source of life and give one another the overflow. I pray that starts with you.

Both singleness and marriage are temporary. In the gospel of Mark we read, "When the dead rise, they will neither marry nor be given in marriage; they will be like the angels in heaven" (Mark 12:25). Pastor Vaughan Roberts reminds us that the pain of a difficult marriage and the pain of singleness will not last forever:

Many who are presently single will one day marry. Others will remain single throughout their lives. But no Christian is single forever. Human marriage reflects the marriage God wants to enjoy with his people forever. The Bible speaks of Jesus as the bridegroom who will one day return to take his bride, the church, to be with him in the perfect new creation. On that day all pain will disappear, including the pain of a difficult marriage or singleness. God will wipe away every tear from our eyes and a great shout will be heard: "Let us rejoice and be glad and give him glory! For the wedding of the Lamb has come, and his bride has made herself ready" (Rev. 7:17; 19:7).[20]

Take charge of your season of life, whether single or married. Don't look to another person to fill what only Jesus can. Relationship formation flows from the inside out. Your character determines everything. Your character creates compatibility and chemistry. Know who you are and the purpose of the season God has you in right now.

EMPOWERING EVERYONE IN THE HOME

Singles: Jesus, not the person you are waiting to marry, is your source of life. Prioritize character development over the similarities and differences of a potential mate. Make sure your list of qualities in a spouse begins with character, not chemistry. Also, make sure your list is not so detailed and close to perfection that you exclude all potential candidates.

Spouses: Jesus, not your spouse, is your source of life. Create compatibility by identifying and developing necessary life negotiation skills. Don't fall for the lie that says, "There's someone more compatible with you out there somewhere." Instead, create compatibility with the one you are committed to in marriage.

Parents: Begin teaching your kids how to form relationships at an early age. Some parents think the best way to do this is to teach kids to avoid relationships altogether. We want to teach our children how to effectively and appropriately express their emotions, not stuff them. Model character for your kids.

FAMILY CONVERSATION STARTERS

1. How would you define compatibility?

2. What are some ways a couple builds compatibility in marriage?

3. Mom and Dad: Share details from your wedding with your children. What was the best part? What would you change?

4. Take some time to picture a special future with your children. Dream with them about their weddings. Write down the details so you have something to share at their weddings years from now.

5. How does marriage solve the problems of isolation and loneliness?

6. What are some ways marriage bears the image of God to the world?

7. Why should children learn about relationship formation at such an early age?

CHAPTER 7

LEAVING HOME

CUTTING THE STRINGS RELATIONALLY, EMOTIONALLY, AND FINANCIALLY

"We ask eighteen-year-olds to make huge decisions about their career and future, when a month ago they had to ask to go to the bathroom."

—ADAM KOTSKO

I never planned on it, but eradicating prolonged adolescence and helping teens launch into adulthood has become a passion of my ministry. So much so that I catch myself going outside the box to help young people embrace responsibility.

In a sermon a few years back, I challenged the young men in our church to date. Many of them read a popular book that told them to stop dating, and they took that message literally. With too many young men finding their adventure in video games and their romance in pornography, I became burdened to help them break that destructive cycle. My message was simple: Leave home, get a job, take responsibility for your life, and find a wife. At one point I even offered to pay for first dates.

The sermon caused quite a stir. One senior lady in our church was so encouraged by the message she wrote me and asked that I preach with similar fervor towards the older men. I took her advice and challenged the senior men the next month.

This sermon bled over into a convocation message I gave at my alma mater, Liberty University. It wasn't planned, but in the middle of my challenge to the young men I was heckled by a female student. It was so shocking that I paused and asked, "Who was that?" The young lady had no problem identifying herself before the 9,000 students. She wanted someone to ask her out on a date.

With her picture on the big screen, I asked the student body, "Is there a young man in here who would ask her out if I paid for your first date?" A young man on the other side of the Vines Center stood up and agreed to be the one. It was a beautiful, spontaneous moment. I wish I could tell you that it had a happy ending, but sources told me later that they dated a couple of times then called it off.

Why are pastors and church leaders not encouraging and promoting marriage to young people? I find this quite troubling. In my years as a student at Liberty University, Dr. Jerry Falwell preached every Wednesday in convocation. He's been with the Lord for many years now, but I have such fond memories of his regular challenge to date and prepare for marriage while in college. Many joked and called this the "ring by Spring" message. Dr. Falwell called us champions for Christ because he believed we could marry, start families, get jobs, and serve the Lord all at the same time. His preaching and teaching gave me the courage to pursue Amy Freitag.

Within two weeks of my college graduation, I asked her to be my wife. She said, "Yes."

Pastors, professors, deans, and resident assistants are additional voices in the life of your child promoting what we assume is taught in the home. Parents are the primary voice for preparing their children to leave home. That preparation starts at an early age. As one pastor recently stated, "If you want a responsible sixteen year old, start teaching them responsibility at age six and give them ten years to practice."

> *Parents must send children out of the home as adults, not on a journey to become one.*

Leaving home as an adult prepared for marriage and family is at the heart of Genesis 2:24: "That is why a man leaves his father and mother and is united to his wife, and they become one flesh." These words, first given in the garden of Eden, were given to a couple with no parents. This is a parenting and marriage verse. Parents must send children out of the home as adults, not on a journey to become one.

The emphasis of Genesis 2:24 is a young man leaving home, immediately marrying, and starting a family. However, today young people leave home and live single for longer periods of time. This increasing gap between leaving and cleaving is a new trend.

Historically and biblically, there are only two phases to life: childhood and adulthood. The apostle Paul explained the transition from childhood to manhood when he wrote, "When I was a child, I talked like a child, I thought like a child, I reasoned like a child. When I became a man, I put the ways of childhood behind me" (1 Corinthians 13:11).

Traditionally, going from a child to an adult meant: (1) leaving home; (2) completing education; (3) finding employment; (4) getting married; and (5) starting a family. Past generations transitioned through these five milestones quickly, if not simultaneously. There was no prolonged track for entering into adulthood. You left home prepared for the responsibility of work, wife, and the world.

LEAVING HOME AND ERADICATING PROLONGED ADOLESCENCE

Adolescence starts in the early teen years and for some continues on into the thirties and forties. Prolonged adolescence is an extended vacation from responsibility. Marriage is a huge responsibility, and many people delay it to party more, drink more, enjoy more lovers, achieve high scores on their favorite video games, make money, get established in a good job, and enjoy their freedom.

Whenever I speak at parenting conferences on prolonged adolescence, there's always that moment when a mom or dad thinks, "Oh my, not only am I raising prolonged adolescents, I'm married to one!" An even better realization is "Oh my, *I* am a prolonged adolescent." Marriages struggle when husband, wife, or both live with too much privilege and not enough responsibility.

Invented in 1904, the term *adolescence* stems from the Latin *adolescere*, which means "to grow up." This age is a period of time when a person is no longer a child but not yet an adult. I call it limbo. Others call it adolescence. I don't argue much with counselors and psychologists on adolescence, but I vehemently fight against prolonged adolescence. It destroys marriages. When a spouse chooses to live as a child, the marriage and family suffer.

From the time God spoke Genesis 2:24 and through the first several thousand years of human history, kids grew up and became adults. There was no intermediate state of being. It's only been in the past one hundred years or so that we've inserted this ten-to-fifteen-year stretch between childhood and adulthood. The Bible uses only the terms *child* and *man*. Biblically, there is no gap between the two. Children become adults.

Prolonged adolescence sends children out of the kid-centered home into the world, telling them to live for themselves for another five to ten years. With our actions we say, "You were raised in a home that revolved around you, your academics, and your athletics; now you need to spend some more time living for yourself." What? We even have a term for it. We call it *independence.* "Go, live by yourself and for yourself for a time before you pursue marriage and family." "Independence" has become a socially acceptable term for "selfishness."

The kid-centered home, combined with an extended period of independence after leaving home, causes some spouses to want to maintain a single lifestyle. Leaving home and cleaving to your spouse means prioritizing your spouse above nights out with friends, hours in front of the television or video games, and excessive participation in hobbies or sporting activities. As a pastor I've seen this play out in one of two ways. One, a spouse never is able to break free from the single lifestyle. Two, the marriage starts out with oneness, but later one or both spouses feels like they missed out on something and they revert to the single lifestyle. In either case, prolonged adolescence fosters the single lifestyle over oneness in marriage.

We've prolonged adolescence to the point that researchers have coined a new term for the gap between adolescence and adulthood. James Cote at the University of Western Ontario coined the term "youthhood." Seriously? We don't need another gap. We need every additional voice in your child's life championing the cause of diminishing privilege with increasing responsibility.

As a pastor, I've hired many college graduates to serve at our church, and many of these young people have frustrated me considerably. I used to think that twenty-somethings were lazy and disrespectful of authority. I've come to learn that many times I'm the first person to challenge them out of adolescence and into adulthood. As their first full-time employer, I'm asked to do what their parents should have done.

Becoming an adult means leaving home, making wise adult decisions, and taking charge of the decisions' outcomes. Parents wait too long to teach their kids to be adults, and as a result, intentionally or unintentionally, they're prolonging the journey into adulthood.

Your child will experience some life events they're not fully prepared for, and that's part of life.

Were you raised in a kid-centered home? If so, don't stress out. If you grew up in a home where Mom and Dad handed you privilege and withheld responsibility, there's still something you can do about it. You can choose to leave the home of privilege and begin valuing responsibility. You can begin to see privilege as something you gain after a season of responsibility. This is a choice you can and must make. Your marriage depends on it.

Our home defines maturity as "knowing I will not be with Mom and Dad forever and planning accordingly." Taking charge of your life means separating well from Mom and Dad. Separation is more of a process than an event. Dropping off a child at college may feel like an event, but years were invested in that day. Every parent struggles with the question, "Did I do a good enough job?" Offer yourself some grace with the answer. Your child will experience some life events they're not fully prepared for, and that's part of life. Good parenting allows them some room to breathe, make some mistakes, and learn some lifelong valuable lessons. Part of adulthood is making decisions and living with the outcomes.

LEAVE HOME FINANCIALLY

Do you have adult children still calling home asking for money?

Does your son or daughter have expectations to upgrade their technology regularly?

Are there expectations for Mom and Dad to pay expenses after the children leave home?

Do you have a thirty year old living in your basement with Star Wars bed sheets on his bed? If so, it's time to cut the strings financially.

Leaving home requires severing your dependence on what your parents provide for you. Your parents should not be buying your clothes, paying your mobile phone plan, or sending you an allowance if you are forty years old. The sooner you establish your financial independence the better.

If you make $30,000 a year and you are married with children, you can't afford to keep up with the latest gadgets and technology.

After food, shelter, clothing, schooling, and transportation, there's not enough money left over to get the upgraded iPhone, iPad, or Macbook. Your kids will require formula, diapers, and the occasional trip to the dentist. Be content with your old technology and avoid upgrades whenever possible.

Entitlement makes us want in a few years what our parents spent a lifetime accumulating. If all your vacations, food, school, cars, insurance, and spending money were handed to you by your parents, it makes it quite difficult to lower your tastes and expectations to meet your current income. It's hard, but doable. Making the necessary budget cuts flows from your character.

Often I share with young husbands who desire to live high on the hog financially, "In your twenties you need to work as many jobs as necessary to get forty or fifty hours a week, and if that doesn't pay the bills, you'll need to work more than fifty hours a week. You have the energy and the time. Make it happen."

Marriage is far more affordable than most people think. Give me a couple of minutes with your weekly budget, and I'll show you.

Here is the simplest equation I know for leaving home financially: hard work + moderate spending = resources to start completing adulthood milestones. In other words, produce more than you consume and stop reaching for handouts from your mom and dad.

The satisfaction you receive from earning and cashing your own paycheck builds confidence for your future. Find joy in earning more than spending, and you'll appreciate life more. When you provide for your own expenses, you become more grateful for what Mom and Dad provided during your childhood. Leaving home requires a strong work ethic. Paying your own way is the fast track to adulthood.

LEAVE HOME RELATIONALLY AND EMOTIONALLY

Leaving home physically and financially is easier to measure than leaving home relationally and emotionally. Once you leave home and begin paying your own bills, you can still find yourself making decisions and "doing life" like you did as a kid. Even though your parents aren't present and speaking into the decisions, you still hear their voice of influence. Mom and Dad spent the majority of your life writing messages on your heart. These messages are present for every discussion you have with your spouse.

While couples regularly point to finances as the source of marital strain, their emotional and relational connection to home drives more of the marriage than most know. This includes the way they earn, give, save, and spend money. Part of my premarital counseling with couples always includes the following eight helps for promoting oneness in marriage, fostering healthy relationships with parents, and leaving home relationally and emotionally.

1. Prioritize your spouse over your parents.

Leaving home starts with understanding the proper bond between parent and child. The bond between a husband and a wife is stronger than the bond between a parent and a child. Your mom and dad love you and want to be involved in your life. The question becomes "How much should they be involved?" Your spouse needs to be the first go-to person on all decision-making, parenting plans, personal struggles, and conflict resolution.

Marriage is a priority relationship that trumps your relationship with your parents. It trumps all other relationships. When you see the word *leave* in Genesis 2:24 you may think you need to move a thousand miles away from Mom and Dad. While there are some cases where that's beneficial, it isn't always necessary. The focus of this text is not geographical. Most newly married couples live close to their parents and move away later in life. The focus of this text is relational and emotional.

Marriage is a priority relationship that trumps your relationship with your parents. It trumps all other relationships.

"Leave" conveys the idea that no relationship, apart from your relationship with God, is more important than your marriage. Your spouse, not your parent, is your new priority relationship.

2. Make decisions with your spouse as a united front.

While parents can be a source of support and encouragement, you must never allow them to be a controlling factor in your decision making. Your relationship with your parents must be free of the expectation to take responsibility for their feelings and actions. Leaving your parents relationally and emotionally means you leave and abandon their expectations for your life and the decisions that affect it. Make your own decisions on vacations, activities, raising your children, career, and joining a certain denominational church. This doesn't mean you block your parents' input forever and always. Nothing honors a parent more than to be asked, "Dad, we were thinking about getting a new car, do you have any suggestions on make or model?" or "Mom, what did you do when one of us kids had a cold that lasted longer than three days?" There's nothing wrong with asking the questions. Keep in mind, it doesn't mean you must follow through with their answers. With those questions, you're simply involving them in your life in a healthy way.

3. When you disagree with your spouse, avoid bringing your parent into the conversation.

Your parent needs to be an ally and advocate for your marriage, not just your opinion. When in conflict, give yourself a time-out and be alone with the Lord. You don't need to call home.

Healthy parents know how to advocate for the marriage, not just the spouse. However, some parents may choose to side with their child and make statements like, "You deserve better." "No one should have to put up with that." "It's not your fault." "You've tried everything to make it work." Don't allow a parent to plant seeds of doubt.

4. Never compare your spouse to a parent.

It's as simple as statements like, "When my mom makes meatloaf, she uses brown gravy, not ketchup," "My dad changes his own oil," or "My parents get a live Christmas tree every year." Unspoken expectations over meal preparations, car maintenance, and household chores can grate on a spouse over time. How your parent handles certain situations may differ from the way your spouse handles it, and that's okay.

Sometimes parents place pressure on you to conform to their traditions, schedules, and gatherings. Part of marriage is creating new traditions and routines. Don't conform your marriage to your parents.

5. Don't take charge of your parents' hearts.

You aren't responsible for their emotions, words, or actions. Trying to change them won't work. Every attempt to change them will exhaust you. Let them be for the sake of your health and marriage. The bond you have with your parents becomes unhealthy when you start making decisions and moving forward in your marriage with these questions in the back of your mind: "What will Dad say if he knows you are leaving the company?" "How will Mom react if we decide to take a vacation this Christmas rather than going home for a visit?" You can love, honor, and bless your parents without taking charge of their hearts.

6. Forgive your parents for everything.

Harboring unresolved anger is like drinking poison and expecting your parent to get sick. You never bury anger dead. It will resurface. If you leave home with anger in your heart towards a parent, it will resurface in your marriage.

You can't change your parents, but you can forgive them. You can't relive your childhood and change your mom and dad. You have zero responsibility for the way you were raised. You can choose to take 100 percent responsibility for your own heart and decide what to do with the hurt and the past.

There's a dad in our church who often says to me, "Ted, don't move off of this point of forgiving your parents. I have adult children who won't speak to me because of the pain I have caused. I'm so sorry. I want them to know the work that Christ has done in me. Their anger hurts everyone, including the grandchildren." If you are that adult child, I beg you to "Forgive as Christ forgave you" (Colossians 3:13). Christ forgives us so we can forgive others, including our parents. I don't ask that you find the strength deep down inside. I ask that you turn to Christ, the only true source of forgiveness.

7. Spend time with your parents.

The Lord convicted me of this a few months back. I was running at a pace that had too many people vying for the little margin I had in the tank. I told my dad after an emotional Sunday morning service, "Dad, one of the reasons I'm slowing down my pace is so I can be a better son." My dad reassured me that he didn't feel neglected, but I know his response was geared towards helping me in that moment of tearful regret.

Schedule regular times for the grandchildren to be with their grandparents. Family means more than anything else to most parents. One way we honor them is to prioritize quality time with them. "Cutting the strings" with home does *not* mean isolating yourselves from them. Be involved in their lives and let them be involved in yours.

8. Stop obeying but never stop honoring your parents.

When you are young and living at home, you are commanded to obey your parents. Ephesians 6:1-3 says, "Children, obey your parents in the Lord, for this is right. 'Honor your father and mother'—which is the first commandment with a promise—'so that it may go well with you and that you may enjoy long life on the earth.'" Children obey. Adult children honor. Obedience ends, but honor never does.

Honor means to esteem as highly valuable. Honor your parents by calling home and thanking them for a life lesson they taught you as a kid. Since you have left home financially, pay for their meal the next time you eat out with them. I know what you are thinking,

"They have way more money than I do, so it makes more sense that they pay." That's not the point. Pay to show honor. Instead of buying your mom another sweater or your dad another ratchet set for a birthday, write them a blessing and share it before family and friends at the next family holiday.

Honor your parents by calling home and thanking them for a life lesson they taught you as a kid.

For her sixty-fourth birthday, we took my mom to the Sunday brunch at the Chateau on the Lake here in Branson. The dining room is full, the food is spread, and a senior adult pianist plays tunes. It's the perfect atmosphere for celebrating a birthday.

About halfway through the meal I asked each member of our family to share something extra special about Pama. (That's what our kids call her.) The request alone brought tears to her eyes. As we worked our way around the table, here is what we shared:

1. She always thinks of the needs of others, not her own.

2. She forgets nothing! She has a file in her brain on every family member and friend. When you share something with her, post on Facebook, etc., she never forgets it. Then when she shops, she looks for what she can buy that person based on their desires, not hers. She buys nothing for herself. She sees it as a waste of money. For example, she labored for years before buying a new phone and computer.

3. Bottom line: She's the most giving person I know.

4. She's our family historian. She's taking over this role from my grandma, Mary Jane Ludwig. Her strongest desire is to keep her family connected. I've lost count of how many times she calls my brother, hands me the phone, and says, "Here, talk to your brother."

5. She loves small children and is a grandma to many. I'm blown away by her capacity for relationships. Her social calendar exhausts me. I can't keep up.

See now why $25 gift cards are fleeting? When we speak words of blessing over our parents it's like a huge gust of wind blowing into a sail. Our parents want to know they did a good job. Your time with family may be limited, so make the most of it.

THE WEDDING AND SEPARATION

Honoring your parents after you leave home recognizes that they raised you, fed you, schooled you, and clothed you. Honor says, "Thank you." They need to acknowledge your rite of passage into adulthood and marriage just as much as you need to praise them for their investment in your life. You left their home and are now starting your own. This is why I enjoy weddings. They are the culmination of honor, separation, and new beginnings.

"Who gives this woman to be married to this man?" is the most emotional question asked at a wedding.

"Her mother and I," is the scripted answer.

After I receive his answer, I ask Dad to turn, face his daughter, and speak a blessing over her. At the rehearsal the night before,

I prep Dad by encouraging him to take his time at this moment, "We're not in a hurry. You are not on the clock. Take your time. You won't have a microphone. This is a special moment between you and your daughter."

Without exception, every dad whimpers and cries his way through the entire blessing.

Gathered guests hear every sniffle. Family and friends who had no plans of crying reach for tissues. After Dad blesses his daughter with spoken words of high value, he turns and speaks a blessing over the groom.

Then, Dad gives his daughter's hand to the groom, steps back, and takes a seat. This is called "Cutting the Strings." This intentional and strategic separation between parent and child is the key to initiating the bond between husband and wife.

I love it when a mom comes up to me at a wedding and says, "I don't feel like I'm losing a daughter today, I feel like I'm gaining a son."

My answer is always the same, "Nope, you're losing a daughter." Of course, that is said with extreme exaggeration to make the point that parents need to back off and allow the new marriage to thrive. Meddling erodes the forever-bond.

In my eighteen years as pastor, I've only had one dad who rebelled against giving the bride at a wedding. We were on schedule and everyone was in their places. The dad walked his daughter down the aisle, stopped at the front, and the groom stepped beside him. I welcomed family and friends, prayed, then asked, "Who gives this woman to be married to this man?" Dad was silent.

Thinking he didn't hear me, I repeated the question, "Who gives this woman to be married to this man?" Dad remained silent.

With a deeper voice and greater strength, I asked a third and final time, "Who gives this woman to be married to this man?"

Dad answered, "I won't give her, but I'll share her." With that, I declared the wedding over. A startled groom looked at me with eyes that said, "This has to happen!" I told him, "We can't go on until Dad gives you his daughter."

Thankfully, the dad submitted to the authority of the church and released his daughter.

At that moment of marriage, Dad and Mom step away, cut the strings, and become backup singers to their child's duet.

EMPOWERING EVERYONE IN THE HOME

Singles: Cutting the strings relationally, emotionally, and financially is the first step to taking charge of adulthood milestones. Create healthy boundaries with your parents by initiating healthy conversations.

Spouses: Make your spouse the priority relationship over your parents. When in conflict, don't call home looking for allies. Don't ask your parents to pick sides. Instead, ask them to advocate for your marriage.

Parents: Prepare your children to leave home as adults, rather than sending them on a journey to become one. Give your adult children room to breathe. Allow them to make decisions early and deal with the consequences of those decisions.

FAMILY CONVERSATION STARTERS

1. What is your favorite part of the wedding?
2. Why is it painful for some parents to "cut the strings"?
3. Why is it painful for adult children to "cut the strings"?
4. How can a parent best "cut the strings"?
5. How can an adult child most effectively communicate with parents over the issue of physical, relational, emotional, and financial separation?

6. What are some ways an adult child honors his or her parents?

7. How often should you call home or go home for a visit?

CHAPTER 8

SINGING BACKUP

SUPPORTING THE MARRIAGES IN YOUR FAMILY

"I believe the home and marriage is the foundation
of our society and must be protected."

—BILLY GRAHAM

When you drive down the road and listen to music, do you turn it up and pretend you're the artist? I do, and I frequently receive strange looks from oncoming traffic. Have you ever pretended you're behind the artist as a backup singer? I have. My steering wheel serves as the drum set.

At Woodland Hills Family Church, we believe every marriage is a duet. Every marriage is the blending of two sets of lyrics into one song. Each spouse brings their lyrics, and the marriage creates the music.

Every marriage is a duet that stirs emotions in others. You've been around couples who leave you thinking, *That was painful.*

That was exhausting. That was heavy metal. That was not good. I don't think they like each other.

You've also been around the couples who, when you leave their presence, you think, *That couple was refreshing. What can we do to be around that couple more? What can we do to have a marriage that looks like theirs?*

What emotions does your marriage stir in others? Are you the "run from couple" or the "run to couple"?

The Song of Songs is a book in the Bible written as a duet. Solomon, the shepherd king, brings his lyrics, and the Shullamite woman brings her lyrics. The Song of Songs is the ultimate duet. There's a group of backup singers in this book called the daughters of Jerusalem. They sing from the background and add harmony to the marriage duet.

Every marriage is a duet that needs backup singers harmonizing from the background.

Every marriage is a duet that needs backup singers harmonizing from the background. When you look up the word *harmony* in the dictionary it says, "Harmony is the combination of simultaneously sounded musical notes to produce chords and chord progressions, having a pleasing affect."[21] That's what good backup singers do. They remain in the background. The spotlight is not on them, but their voices add to the duet. They enhance the duet and make it pleasing.

The first time we "hear" the backup singers in the Song of Songs is in chapter 1, verse 4 right after the Shullamite woman expresses deep, sexual desire for Solomon. They don't shut her down or tell her to stop feeling that way before the wedding, which comes in chapter 3. No, they rejoice with her: "We rejoice and delight in you; we will praise your love more than wine."

"Rejoice and delight" mean "a spontaneous expression of excitement and cheer." We feel this at weddings when a pastor says, "I now pronounce you husband and wife." The same excitement hits us when the pastor says, "You may kiss the bride." A final expression of cheer erupts when the pastor steps to the side of the couple and pronounces them Mr. and Mrs. The music plays, and the couple gets their groove on down the aisle.

Is it possible to have a marriage that people still rejoice over ten, twenty, or thirty years after the wedding? I believe so. Amy and I want to be the couple that when you leave our home or presence you say, "We want that too."

"Praise" in Song of Songs 1:4 means "an expression of gratefulness for a past event." To paraphrase the daughters of Jerusalem, "We praise your love for each other. When we think about your love, it gladdens our hearts. We are giddy for you." Why is it important to have people like this in your life? The answer is simple. The day may come where your love and excitement for each other wanes. As time goes by, this happens. Happy couples and divorced couples share the same level of marital satisfaction on the day of their wedding. Backup singers help us stay true to our vows. We need to be reminded and held accountable to the joy we committed to. An expression of gratefulness for a past event says, "I go back to your wedding, and I remember the joy you had and I'm grateful for it. I will praise that. I will cheer for that for years to come."

WHO BRINGS HARMONY TO YOUR MARRIAGE?

Start right now by thinking about the backup singers in your life. These are people who bring great harmony to your marriage, and you need to turn up the volume on them. You need to hear from them more.

This past summer our youth went to summer camp. Upon their return, I asked them for their greatest take-away from the week. They told me the speaker taught on voices. We all have voices in our lives, and some of us have too many voices speaking into our lives. There are some voices we need to turn down, and there are some we need to mute altogether. In other words, unfriend or block those who want to lead you astray. Then there are other voices you need to turn way up and pay attention to.

> *Great backup singers point us in a direction that leads to health, not death or destruction.*

Singles need backup singers who honor, enjoy, and prioritize marriage. They need to mute those who dishonor marriage. You need to mute the voices who say you should never get married because it's just too risky. Mute the ones who run down your boyfriends or girlfriends. Mute the ones who mock their spouses. If someone is leading your potential duet off-key, mute them.

My wife recently confronted a friend going through a struggling marriage. She encouraged her friend to be careful who she called after a fight. Amy said, "You called that person because you knew she would validate the decision you're thinking about right now. You wanted someone to validate this decision even though you know this is not the right decision. You need truth spoken into your life. Call people who will advocate for marriage and personal responsibility." We need backup singers who will tell us what we need to hear, not what we want to hear. Great backup singers point us in a direction that leads to health, not death or destruction.

Parents with adult children in struggling marriages find themselves as backup singers whether they desire it or not. They get to choose what type of backup singer they want to be. I've seen the pain on parents' faces as they struggle with a child's broken marriage. They say, "We need to stay out of it and let them figure it out." I'm all for boundaries, but I think there is much a parent can do to strengthen their child's marriage without violating the "leave and cleave" emphasis of Scripture.

BACKING UP YOUR CHILD'S MARRIAGE

Here are three ways a parent can "cut the strings" and slip into the background as a backup singer:

1. Advocate for the couple, not just your child.
If your child calls after a fight, seeking your validation, do more listening and understanding than instructing. Be careful not to add new lyrics to the song. Instead, remind them of the joy they have experienced throughout their marriage. Go to the lyrics of exclusivity. Remind them of the positives and the good words they can speak over each other.

It's tempting to become an ally for just your child. Now of course, I'm not speaking of an adult child in an abusive marriage. In that case you most definitely advocate and protect your child at all costs.

2. Guard your heart from treating your child as a victim.

Again, I'm not speaking of physically, emotionally, or verbally abusive marriages. Helping your child take charge of their words and actions is difficult, but you need to avoid the position where you tell your child their spouse is the one with the problems. Good counselors focus on the person right in front of them and guard against bashing those who are absent. Don't contribute to a bashing session. Speak life and truth over both spouses.

3. Leverage weddings, holidays, and anniversaries.

I heard from a young woman in Phoenix, Arizona, of a creative way her parents leveraged the holidays for their children's marriages. She had many siblings, all of whom were married. Their mom and dad asked each couple to plan the perfect date and bring the plans home for the holidays. They would each get a turn to explain their perfect date and everyone would vote on the most creative. I love this. The most creative date won a big prize. Now those are parents seeking ways to advocate in the marriages of their children. We need more of that.

Recently, my friend Corey Mitchell and I designed a greeting card we simply call the More Than Wine card. "We rejoice and delight in you, we will praise your love more than wine," is on the cover. On the inside it reads, "I want to speak words of high value over your marriage. Your marriage is important to me." To the right of that it says, "I rejoice . . . I delight . . . I praise . . ." There is plenty of space to personalize a message.

Have you ever noticed that birthday cards and anniversary cards all have the same tone? The tone is, "You made it!" How wonderful would it be to receive a card celebrating twenty-five years of marriage that said, "You endured and pushed through, congratulations!"

The More Than Wine card is more than an anniversary or wedding card. It's a marriage card meant to bless the marriages around you. There are many ways we ask our congregation to use these cards and it starts at the wedding.

When you come to a wedding at Woodland Hills, every guest receives the More Than Wine card. After the processional, everyone takes their seats as I step to the side of the bride and groom. You've no doubt been to a wedding, so you know what comes next: "Family and friends, we are gathered here today to witness the union of Jeremy and Jessica." After a few welcome statements, we move to the giving of the bride.

Let me encourage you to slow down the welcome and give it some real meaning. Here is what we say about the More Than Wine card at Woodland Hills:

"Friends and family, you and I are a part of a very special moment in the life of this couple. Today, they leave home and become one. You are here for a specific purpose. We ask that you witness the exchange of their vows, pray for this couple, speak words of high honor over this couple, and hold them accountable to their commitment.

You received a card on your way in today. That card is your opportunity to rejoice, delight, and praise the love and marriage of this couple.

As they exchange their vows, there are going to be moments in the ceremony that spark in you an "aw" or maybe even a "wahoo." Write these down. Write down their expressions, words, glances, and movements. You are like reporters, capturing their every move. This is an opportunity for you to show gratefulness for what God is doing in this couple.

There are three ways you can use this card.

First, we ask that some of you place your card in the More Than Wine box at the reception. Throughout their first year of marriage, they will reach into that box and pull out cards from time to time to be encouraged with what you spoke over them at their wedding.

Second, we ask that some of you take this card with you and send it to the couple on their first anniversary. That's why we included the envelope. What a joyous time for a newlywed couple to go out to the mailbox around their first anniversary and receive cards from dozens of backup singers.

Third, this group includes the wedding party, parents, grandparents, and close friends. We ask you to make a bold promise. Hold onto this card and send it to the couple at the first signs of trouble. If you hear this couple is considering divorce or separation, send them the card. If you meet them and can feel tension in their relationship, send the card. If there appears to be distance between them, send the card. You have the couple's permission to do so.

We want to bless this marriage."

The third suggestion often raises eyebrows. "What did he say? Is it really our place to hold them accountable to their vows? I don't want to lose a friend over this." Yes, it is your place. Bless the couple with your words. Be bold. Take charge. Hold them accountable.

HELPING A MARRIAGE IN CRISIS HAS CHALLENGES

Helping a struggling marriage is challenging, but let me encourage you to take the risk. Bless your children, siblings, parents, and friends in their marriages. You may feel you need to stay out of it and let them work it out. At that point, what do you have to lose? What do you have to lose as your kids begin to separate and divorce? I know many parents and family members who do nothing because they don't know what to do. They don't know where to take it. Don't let insecurities and fears keep you from advocating for the marriage.

Helping a struggling marriage is challenging, but let me encourage you to take the risk.

Don't let attacks on your past attempts keep you from reaching out now and in the future. Continue to back up their marriage. Don't let reminders of your past mistakes keep you from trying again. Do you remember when you got into conflict years ago and harsh words were exchanged? God's mercies are new every day. Don't let that keep you from starting to do the right thing now.

Don't let anger from a hurting family member keep you from loving and caring for them. You will experience this. They may say, "It's none of your business!" "Butt out!" "Mind your own business." Don't let that keep you from loving and caring for them. Go after them.

WHERE DO YOU START AND WHAT DO YOU SAY?

Use a card, note, email, phone call, or text to speak words of high value over your friends and family. Above all those, I encourage you to get face-to-face. Here are some words of high honor to back up the marriages around you:

- I desire to bless your marriage by speaking words of high value over both of you. Your marriage is important to me.
- I rejoice in how you prioritize your marriage by spending quality time together.
- I love that you take a date night every week and anything we can do to help you with that date night, let us be a part of it. Bring the kids over; we would love to be a part of it.
- I delight in the way you speak highly of each other in public.
- We went out to dinner a couple months ago and when you held the door open for her and just the little pet names you call her; I love that. When I see that, it does something in me; it stirs emotions in me; it causes me to rejoice and to cheer.
- I praise your love and the commitment to your vows.

- I know it hasn't been an easy season and I know it's been challenging. I know what you're going through with your son or with your daughter is tough and I know how much you love him and I know how much he or she is draining on the family right now and that you are kind of centered around that right now, but I just want you to know I'm proud of you through the difficult times for staying true to your vows.

- I rejoice in knowing you will be together until one of you lays the other in the arms of Jesus or until the Lord returns.

- I delight in how you accept one another's goals, dreams, and plans for the future.

- I praise the example you have set for your children and your grandchildren.

- I rejoice in how you enjoy life together.

- I delight in how you esteem each other as highly valuable.

When people think about your marriage, do they praise your love? Who are your backup singers? Some of you need backup singers in your lives. You need backup singers who move you towards the Lord, not away from Him. You need backup singers who move you towards your commitment in marriage, not away from it. You need backup singers who will teach you and bless you as you honor, enjoy, and prioritize marriage even through difficult seasons.

One of the greatest words I hear on a daily basis is "Daddy." My tween daughter still calls me "Daddy." I hope that never changes.

One day I will stand with her at the back of a church looking down the aisle at her soon-to-be husband. It's on that day that I hope to hear, "Daddy, thank you for loving Mom. You showed me how a wife should be treated."

Mom and Dad, may your marriage be an example of the gospel of Jesus, giving to one another, sacrificing for one another. Let your children look to you as their first backup singers. Let your children rejoice, delight, and praise the love of your marriage.

THE DOUBLE DATE

Do you know a married couple who inspires you? Find another couple that stirs good emotions in you and invite them on a date.

It's important to learn from older, wiser couples. If you are a mom who has antibacterial product hanging on your purse, you need to find a mom who watched her kids pick up cigarette butts and chew on them. She called it roughage. Past generations went on vacations and let their kids sleep in the back window of the car. Today, we strap our kids in like we're launching them into outer space. Our parents' generation used a contraption called the playpen. They placed a few kids in there with only one toy. I think it's where we got the idea for cage fighting. When Mom needed to work in another room of the house, she dragged the playpen into the room with her. Kids learned to play with others and to entertain themselves. I've heard of extreme cases where children tried crawling out of the playpen and Mom turned the playpen upside down to contain them.

> *It's important to learn from older, wiser couples.*

A double date with an experienced couple reminds you that your children will survive and your marriage can thrive. When you allow backup singers into your life, you find the validation, encouragement, and support every marriage needs.

My friend recently sent me a picture of an older couple at a ball game. They both wore matching jerseys. His jersey had the word "together" with the number "19." Hers read "since" with the number "51." As they stood together, from behind, the jerseys read, "Together since 1951." I wish Amy and I could ask that couple out on a date.

Take the following fifty-two questions with you on the date to guide your conversation. (You can download these on our church website at http://woodhills.org/datenightchallenge/.)

1. How did you two meet?

2. How long did you date before you married?

3. Tell us about your wedding. How much did you spend?

4. Who was in your wedding party?

5. Where did you go on your honeymoon?

6. Tell us about your first home. Square footage? Cost?

7. What was your household income that first year?

8. How many jobs have you had during your marriage?

9. What was your worst job?

10. What was your favorite job?

11. How does your generation's work ethic compare to that of ours?

12. Tell us about your kids.

13. What was the hardest part of parenting?

14. What observations/concerns do you have for twenty-first-century parents?

15. Do you believe the days go slow and the years go fast? How so?

16. When did you come to faith in Christ?

17. Who played a significant role in your faith journey?

18. Do you have a life verse?

19. Do you remember a sermon that profoundly impacted your life?

20. Which character in the Bible do you most identify with?

21. How do/will you serve the church in retirement?

22. What is your best childhood memory?

23. Share with us the toughest season of your marriage? What did you learn from that season?

24. What world event most impacted you?

25. Which U.S. president inspires you the most? Why?

26. What is your greatest hope for our generation?

27. What is your greatest fear for our generation?

28. What is your greatest hope for our church?

29. What one issue drove a wedge between you two in the early years of your marriage?

30. Did you prioritize your marriage while raising kids? How or why not?

31. Was there ever a time where you wanted to throw in the towel and give up on marriage?

32. Have family or friends ever discouraged you in your marriage? If so, what did they say? What would you say to them now?

33. Do you have a friend or family member who regularly encourages you in your marriage?

34. Were/are your parents followers of Jesus?

35. How did your parents impact your marriage?

36. To the husband: Is your wife the queen of your home? How do you display this official coronation to your kids?

37. To the wife: In what practical ways do you show respect to your husband on a daily basis?

38. Sexual intimacy: spontaneous or scheduled?

39. Which TV sitcom best represents your marriage and family?

40. Do you have a regular date night? Most creative date?

41. What is the best vacation you've been on as a family?

42. What is the worst vacation you've been on as a family? What would you do differently if you could redo that trip?

43. What are your favorite travel destinations?

44. Do you prefer buffets or gourmet dining?

45. What steps are you taking to care for your health?

46. Describe your dream vacation.

47. How do you make each other laugh?

48. How do you divide household chores?

49. Define your marriage in one sentence.

50. Describe your spouse's personality.

51. What one big dream do you have for your marriage?

52. After _____ years of marriage, what would you say is the #1 secret to a smokin' hot marriage?

EMPOWERING EVERYONE IN THE HOME

Singles: You have an important role to play in honoring the marriages around you. Find ways to bless the couples around you. When you hear a friend is getting married, rejoice with them. Praise the young budding love of your couple friends and encourage them to remain pure and avoid the unnecessary delay of marriage.

Spouses: Think through the recent conversations you have been a part of with family and friends. Who encourages your marriage? Turn them up. Spend some more time around them. Go to them with marital struggles. Who discourages your marriage? Mute them. Don't seek them as allies when things get tough. Avoid those who validate sinful thoughts or desires.

Parents: Whether you are single or married, you can begin preparing and backing up the marriages of your children starting at any age. One way to back up your child's marriage is to not run down the other parent. Don't point the finger of blame at the other person.

FAMILY CONVERSATION STARTERS

1. Do you have a couple in mind you can invite out on a double date? Maybe it's your parents, and at the next family get together you can have the kids ask grandma and grandpa some of the questions. If you do this, be sure to omit question #38.

2. What are some positive statements you can make to encourage someone in their marriage?

3. Do you know someone who needs an encouraging word spoken over their marriage? If so, what should you say or write?

4. Are you open to someone holding you accountable to your vows?

5. Who should you invite into your marriage and family as backup singers?

CHAPTER 9

ENTERING FAMILY

HOW BIRTH, MARRIAGE, AND DEATH
BRING PEOPLE BACK TO CHURCH

*"Sound advice is a beacon, good teaching is a light,
moral discipline is a life path."*

—EUGENE H. PETERSON

H idden in the Ozark Mountains, in the heart of Branson, Missouri, at the west end of Country Music Boulevard, with a wooden roller coaster in the parking lot, there's a castle that Woodland Hills Family Church calls home. We are a young congregation, about thirteen years old, and passionate about marriage and family. All of our environments, programs, events, and messages point singles, children, moms, dads, husbands, wives, grandmas, and grandpas to Jesus.

We planted our church as Woodland Hills Community Church with a desire to reach our community. Five years later, we changed our name to Woodland Hills Family Church with a desire to reach the families in our community. Our new name reflects the DNA of our mission.

Our mission statement reads, "Inspiring the family to become fully devoted followers of Jesus." Our church mirrors our town. I am grateful to live in a community where business owners, entertainers, retirees, workers, government leaders, and families love Jesus. If you go to a show in Branson, more than likely you will hear the gospel. At Silver Dollar City, our theme park, you know that the owners love and live to proclaim the name of Jesus. We minister to millions of tourists a year. I'm grateful that Branson is a place where Jesus and family are unashamedly shouted from the rooftops (and stages).

Helping individuals take charge of their faith and family is at the heart of our message. We exist to equip singles, couples, and parents in their faith and family with the responsibility they will need for work and relationships. Our church is a local body of families of all shapes and sizes.

There are three life events that tend to draw people back to a church family. The birth of a child, the planning of a wedding, and the death of a family member prioritize life for all of us. There's an urge in people to "do it right" and to get the blessing of the Lord over children, marriage, and death. At Woodland Hills Family Church, we celebrate all three.

BIRTH

Our church celebrates birth with baby dedications. We love kids and invest heavily in our programming to lead children into a personal relationship with Jesus and to help them grow in their walk with Him.

We celebrate baby dedications four times a year. We require parents to take a class that emphasizes the church as an additional voice echoing what Mom and Dad are already saying in the home. This requires a shift in thinking for most who take the class. Many assume the primary responsibility of discipling children falls on the church, but we believe that responsibility falls on the shoulders of the parents. Mom and Dad must take charge of their child's discipleship.

Our children's director, Stephanie Watson, gives each family a jar of marbles. There's a marble for each week the parent has left with their child before the child leaves home. At our last dedication, Braxton's parents received a jar with 923 marbles. Caiden's parents received 914 marbles. Kolby's parents received 624.

I joke with the congregation and say, "The purpose of the jar is to show how parenting makes you lose your marbles." No, the real reason for the jar is for parents to grasp that the days go slow, but the weeks, months and years go fast. If I had a jar for Corynn, it would have 344 marbles. Carson's jar would have about 440 marbles. Number the days and weeks you have left. If you don't want to buy $30 worth of marbles, go to the app store and download Legacy Countdown by the Rethink Group. It's a digital marble countdown. This is a great tool to help you make the most of your remaining time with your children.

You've heard the saying, "It takes a village." We believe, "It takes the home and the church."

We challenge parents to be intentional with each marble. Make the most of your time, and our church commits to reinforcing everything you say and do at home. After we give out the jars to the parents with their children standing on the stage, I ask the congregation to stand and pray over the families:

"Father, thank You for breathing life into each one of these children. You are the Creator and Sustainer of all life. We pray for Mom and Dad as they raise these children in the instruction of the Lord. As these children grow and learn about Your Son Jesus Christ, we pray they will place faith in Jesus. As their church family, we commit to support, bless, and pray for Mom and Dad. We also commit to being an additional voice in the life of each child here. We love You and thank You for the future these families have together. Use these families to glorify You."

Children are a blessing and a welcomed addition to the home and church. We value them. The church and home present a united front to the child. You've heard the saying, "It takes a village." We believe, "It takes the home and the church."

MARRIAGE

Our church celebrates and promotes marriage with weddings.

In May 2014, a group of church leaders in Dallas invited me to speak on the subject of weddings. The coordinator of the event heard of my passion for promoting marriage and my love for performing weddings. Over the phone he told me, "Ted, as the executive pastor of our church, I did everything in my power to prevent people from getting married at our church. A large church with limited staff resources and multiple weekend services makes for a very difficult event to turn over."

He's not alone. Many churches, especially large or growing churches, view weddings as a hassle. Even if that isn't in the heart of the pastor or staff, engaged couples sure feel it. Their request to get married at their church is sometimes met with low enthusiasm. We must do something about this. We can't be for marriage and, at the same time, be frustrated by weddings.

> We can't be for marriage and, at the same time, be frustrated by weddings.

If I could do weddings full-time, I would. I love them. My plan is to be a full-time wedding officiant in my sunset years. My passion in life and ministry is showing couples how joy and festivity are more than possible long after the cake is cut. Every wedding is like a mini-marriage conference. It's the perfect time and place to tie the knot, offer hope to struggling marriages, encourage singles, and share the gospel.

Weddings, just like marriage, require thought, planning, and work before you get to the joy and festivity. Whether it's a beach wedding, backyard wedding, or after-Sunday-morning-service wedding, it takes much preparation to pull off the big day. Cost doesn't matter. You can spend a few hundred dollars or several thousand. Either way, you'll need to think through the guest list, invitations, rings, attire, bridesmaids, groomsmen, pastor, flowers, cake, vows, music, photographer, and gift registries. A wedding to-do list is long.

Most brides and some grooms love planning their wedding. I've yet to meet a couple looking forward to the big day with dread. Maybe there are a few family dynamics to work through, but for the most part couples have great anticipation for their wedding day. Here are a few thoughts for you and your church to consider as you rethink and promote weddings within your congregation:

Differentiate between a justice of the peace and a pastor.

I find many couples today desiring a pastor to serve as a justice of the peace. "We have decided to marry and now we want to have a church wedding with you leading it." A justice of the peace has limited legal power to make a marriage official and legitimate. A pastor gives counsel and blessing to a couple.

Differentiate between a wedding coordinator and a pastor.

As the pastor officiating at a wedding, I love encouraging couples, family, and gathered guests. I don't care to be the guy who tells people where to stand, the pace at which they should walk down the aisle, and how they should dress for the camera. Request that a family member or friend fulfill the role of wedding coordinator and allow the pastor to focus on the content of the ceremony.

Work with your receptionist to offer genuine support.

When someone calls the church office and says, "We would like to talk to someone about getting married," train whoever answers the phone to respond with statements like, "Congratulations!" or "When's the big day?" Avoid statements like, "Well, let me see who is available to talk to you" or "We don't host a lot of weddings here because of our weekend services." Part of creating a marriage and family culture at your church is developing a genuine enthusiasm about marriage on the front lines.

Develop relationships with local wedding venues such as chapels, gardens, and resorts.

Give engaged couples options. Our church meets in a castle. You would think that every princess would want her wedding in a castle. However, smack dab in the middle of our auditorium and in the center of the main aisle there is a pole. This makes for an awkward processional. We are glad to work with our brides in an alternate venue of their choice.

Use the wedding as a "link" between premarital and newlywed.

The gap is unintentional, but many churches work with engaged couples and couples in crisis to the exclusion of couples who seem to be doing "okay." Create a newlywed follow-up plan that includes encouraging personal touches within the first year of marriage.

Wordsmith your wedding guidelines to add more grace.

A few years ago, my assistant asked me to reconsider the tone of our wedding guidelines. When someone called the office to seek premarital counseling and to schedule their wedding, we sent them our wedding guidelines. This document included where we stood on cohabitation. We never heard back from many couples. This was not our intent. Tough conversations are better in person, not on print. You don't need to put everything you believe in a policy manual. Don't change what you believe, but get face-to-face with the couple so they can hear your heart and see your genuine love and concern for them.

Give people a clear path through your marriage ministry. Premarital counseling is the perfect time to give the couple a discipleship plan. From church membership to small groups, challenge couples to press into a biblical community. Translate the support of the church for their wedding into even more support for their marriage.

I love it when engaged couples ask us, "What does your church believe about marriage?" The question often leads to discussions about politics or cohabitation. While we don't believe this is an exhaustive list, we wrote a marriage creed with core passages to start the conversation with children, singles, engaged couples, newlyweds, all the way through couples married for fifty years or more. This list makes for great conversations around the family table, in Sunday school classes, and small groups:

1. We want marriage ministry and teaching to be current, not outdated, boring, preachy, or limited to its feminine aspects. We want men to hear "marriage ministry" and not run the other way. In no way, shape, or form do we seek to turn men into women. We celebrate the created gender differences.

So God created mankind in his own image, in the image of God he created them; male and female he created them. (Genesis 1:27)

2. We believe marriage models the gospel of Jesus.

"For this reason a man will leave his father and mother and be united to his wife, and the two will become one flesh." This is a profound mystery—but I am talking about Christ and the church. (Ephesians 5:31–32)

3. We believe Jesus, not a spouse, is a person's source of life and sanctification.

And so we know and rely on the love God has for us.
God is love. Whoever lives in love lives in God, and God in them. This is how love is made complete among us so that we will have confidence on the day of judgment: In this world we are like Jesus. There is no fear in love. But perfect love drives out fear, because fear has to do with punishment. The one who fears is not made perfect in love.
We love because he first loved us. (1 John 4:16–19)

4. We believe marriage is normative and singleness is the exception.

The LORD God said, "It is not good for the man to be alone. I will make a helper suitable for him." (Genesis 2:18)

5. We believe the bond between a husband and wife is to be stronger than the bond between a parent and a child. We seek to eradicate the kid-centered home.

The man said,

"This is now bone of my bones and flesh of my flesh; she shall be called 'woman,' for she was taken out of man."

That is why a man leaves his father and mother and is united to his wife, and they become one flesh. (Genesis 2:23–24)

6. We believe marriage was created by God to be received with thanksgiving.

They forbid people to marry and order them to abstain from certain foods, which God created to be received with thanksgiving by those who believe and who know the truth. (1 Timothy 4:3)

7. We believe children should leave home as adults, not live for an extended period of time on a journey to become one. Historically and biblically there are only two seasons of life: childhood and adulthood. We eradicate prolonged adolescence and prepare our children for adulthood and marriage by prioritizing responsibility over privilege.

That is why a man leaves his father and mother and is united to his wife, and they become one flesh. (Genesis 2:24)

8. We believe spouses should enjoy life and each other. You don't need to choose between life and a wife. You can have both at the same time.

Go, eat your food with gladness, and drink your wine with a joyful heart, for God has already approved what you do. Always be clothed in white, and always anoint your head with oil. Enjoy life with your wife, whom you love, all the days of this meaningless life that God has given you under the sun—all your meaningless days. For this is your lot in life and in your toilsome labor under the sun. (Ecclesiastes 9:7–9)

9. We believe the wife is called to submit to and affirm the leadership of her husband.

Wives, in the same way submit yourselves to your own husbands so that, if any of them do not believe the word, they may be won over without words by the behavior of their wives, when they see the purity and reverence of your lives. Your beauty should not come from outward adornment, such as elaborate hairstyles and the wearing of gold jewelry or fine clothes. Rather, it should be that of your inner self, the unfading beauty of a gentle and quiet spirit, which is of great worth in God's sight. For this is the way the holy women of the past who put their hope in God used to adorn themselves. They submitted themselves to their own husbands, like Sarah, who obeyed Abraham and called him her lord. You are her daughters if you do what is right and do not give way to fear. (1 Peter 3:1–6)

10. We believe the husband is to be the considerate leader of the home.

Husbands, in the same way be considerate as you live with your wives, and treat them with respect as the weaker partner and as heirs with you of the gracious gift of life, so that nothing will hinder your prayers. (1 Peter 3:7)

11. We believe every follower of Jesus should be an advocate for marriage.

We rejoice and delight in you; we will praise your love more than wine. (Song of Songs 1:4b)

12. We teach our children to honor marriage, not just purity.

Marriage should be honored by all, and the marriage bed kept pure, for God will judge the adulterer and all the sexually immoral. (Hebrews 13:4)

13. We believe sex is to be frequent and creative between a husband and wife.

Now for the matters you wrote about: "It is good for a man not to have sexual relations with a woman." But since sexual immorality is occurring, each man should have sexual relations with his own wife, and each woman with her own husband. The husband should fulfill his marital duty to his wife, and likewise the wife to her husband. The wife does not have authority over her own body but yields it to her husband. In the same way, the husband does not have authority over his own body but yields it to his wife. Do not deprive each other except perhaps by mutual consent and for a time, so that you may devote yourselves to prayer. Then come together again so that Satan will not tempt you because of your lack of self-control. (1 Corinthians 7:1–5)

Eat, friends, and drink; drink your fill of love. (Song of Songs 5:1b)

14. We advocate for marriage, not just the spouse.

Where has your beloved gone, most beautiful of women? Which way did your beloved turn, that we may look for him with you? (Song of Songs 6:1)

15. We believe God hates divorce, but loves the divorced person.

"The man who hates and divorces his wife," says the LORD, the God of Israel, "does violence to the one he should protect," says the Lord Almighty.

So be on your guard, and do not be unfaithful. (Malachi 2:16)

16. We believe in the exclusivity of marriage. Spouses must make the choice to give up all other choices.

My beloved is mine and I am his; he browses among the lilies. (Song of Songs 2:16)

17. We believe great marriages flow from character, not chemistry.

Above all else, guard your heart, for everything you do flows from it. (Proverbs 4:23)
> A good name is better than fine perfume. (Ecclesiastes 7:1)

18. We believe that couples must prioritize time together to increase marital satisfaction. We prioritize a daily delay, weekly withdrawal (date night), and an annual abandon.

Daily Delay (in the home)

While the king was at his table, my perfume spread its fragrance.
> My beloved is to me a sachet of myrrh resting between my breasts.
> My beloved is to me a cluster of henna blossoms from the vineyards of En Gedi.
> How beautiful you are, my darling! Oh, how beautiful! Your eyes are doves.
> How handsome you are, my beloved! Oh, how charming! And our bed is verdant.
> The beams of our house are cedars; our rafters are firs. (Song of Songs 1:12–17)

Weekly Withdrawal (on a date away from the home)

Listen! My beloved! Look! Here he comes, leaping across the mountains, bounding over the hills.

My beloved is like a gazelle or a young stag. Look! There he stands behind our wall, gazing through the windows, peering through the lattice.

My beloved spoke and said to me, "Arise, my darling, my beautiful one, come with me.

See! The winter is past; the rains are over and gone.

Flowers appear on the earth; the season of singing has come, the cooing of doves is heard in our land.

The fig tree forms its early fruit; the blossoming vines spread their fragrance.

Arise, come, my darling; my beautiful one, come with me." (Song of Songs 2:8–13)

Annual Abandon (away from home and out of town)

I belong to my beloved, and his desire is for me.

Come, my beloved, let us go to the countryside, let us spend the night in the villages.

Let us go early to the vineyards to see if the vines have budded, if their blossoms have opened, and if the pomegranates are in bloom— there I will give you my love. (Song of Songs 7:10–12)

19. We believe marriage foreshadows the future of every Christian: the wedding of Christ to His bride, the church.

Then I heard what sounded like a great multitude, like the roar of rushing waters and like loud peals of thunder, shouting:

"Hallelujah! For our Lord God Almighty reigns.

Let us rejoice and be glad and give him glory! For the wedding of the Lamb has come, and his bride has made herself ready.

Fine linen, bright and clean, was given her to wear."
(Fine linen stands for the righteous acts of God's holy people.)

Then the angel said to me, "Write this: Blessed are those who are invited to the wedding supper of the Lamb!" And he added, "These are the true words of God."

At this I fell at his feet to worship him. But he said to me, "Don't do that! I am a fellow servant with you and with your brothers and sisters who hold to the testimony of Jesus. Worship God! For it is the Spirit of prophecy who bears testimony to Jesus." (Revelation 19:6–10)

20. We believe marriage is between a man and woman for a lifetime.

They exchanged the truth about God for a lie, and worshiped and served created things rather than the Creator—who is forever praised. Amen.

Because of this, God gave them over to shameful lusts. Even their women exchanged natural sexual relations for unnatural ones. In the same way the men also abandoned natural relations with women and were inflamed with lust for one another. Men committed shameful acts with other men, and received in themselves the due penalty for their error. (Romans 1:25–27)

My prayer for singles, spouses and parents is that, "Marriage should be honored by all" (Hebrews 13:4) and celebrated within the local church. Let's esteem marriage as highly valuable by celebrating and promoting God-ordained matrimony.

DEATH

Our church celebrates life at funerals. When you attend a funeral, life slows down and you start asking good questions. Questions like, "How am I living?" "Am I loving my family well?" "Is Jesus my priority relationship?" These questions are why I start every funeral with Ecclesiastes 7:1–4:

> A good name is better than fine perfume, and the day of death better than the day of birth.
> It is better to go to a house of mourning than to go to a house of feasting, for death is the destiny of everyone; the living should take this to heart.
> Frustration is better than laughter, because a sad face is good for the heart.
> The heart of the wise is in the house of mourning, but the heart of fools is in the house of pleasure.

In the house of mourning, life sinks in. No one ever leaves a party saying, "That changed my life." That's not the purpose of a party. However, you do leave funerals changed.

This past February, Amy and I both lost a grandmother. My grandma, Mary Jane Ludwig, died at age ninety. We had her funeral on a Thursday in Naperville, Illinois. The following Monday, we buried Amy's grandma, Eurlis Kelzenberg, in Owatonna, Minnesota. It was a tough week. We asked many good questions.

My mom is the historian of our family. She inherited this role from her mom. While our family mourns, my mom brings us back to our roots. Through mourning the loss of my grandma, I learned that my great-grandma was a marriage advocate who backed up the duets all around her.

Margaret Louise Brown was born in Jacksonville, Illinois, on November 14, 1895, to Edwin and Erminabelle Brown. She married William J. Cadigan, Jr. in 1916 and they had four children: William J. III, Raymond, Eileen, and Mary Jane.

Margaret was widowed at age sixty and spent the rest of her eighty-eight years helping her children and others. She was a servant to all and enjoyed life to the fullest. She was a very wise woman who helped her children and grandchildren with their studies and tutored friends' children. Math was her specialty, especially Algebra. She had a special way of making everyone feel as though they were her favorite. This is still true among her twenty-two grandchildren. I'm her forty-one-year-old great-grandson, and I remember being her favorite.

> *When you attend a funeral, life slows down and you start asking good questions.*

My grandma, Mary Jane Ludwig, was her youngest daughter. As a boy I would visit grandma's house to see great-grandma sitting in a rocking chair in the corner of the kitchen. I would kneel beside her chair, gently rub her arm, and say, "Grandma, it's Teddy." She smiled and placed her hand on mine.

On the day of my mom and dad's wedding, great-grandma handed my mom a single page of what she called "Good Rules for Marriage." Over forty-five years later, my mom still has the rules framed in her home:

Never both be angry at once.

Never yell at each other unless the house is on fire.

Yield to the wishes of the other as an exercise in self-discipline if you can't think of another reason.

If you have a choice between making yourself or your mate look good, choose your mate.

If you have any criticism, make it lovingly.

Never bring up a mistake of the past.

Neglect the whole world rather than each other.

Never let the day end without saying at least one kind or complimentary thing to your life's partner.

Never meet without an affectionate welcome.

Never let the sun go down on an argument unresolved.

When you do wrong, make sure you have talked it out and asked for forgiveness.

Remember, it takes two to make a quarrel. The one with the least sense is the one who will be doing most the talking.

We learn at funerals. Whether it's something about our family or something about tradition, take the time and mourn. Ask questions that recalibrate your life. This past summer, I learned something about the honor guard at the funerals of our service men and women. Military funerals have a tradition of firing off three shots at the end of the ceremony:

"The three volleys came from an old battlefield custom. The two warring sides would cease hostilities to clear their dead from the battlefield, and the firing of three volleys meant that the dead had been properly cared for and the side was ready to resume the battle."[22]

Once you die, the grind of life (or the battle) continues for your family and friends. Funerals recalibrate your life. What will be said about you when your three shots are fired? What questions will people ask at your funeral? How are you living? What needs to change?

EMPOWERING EVERYONE IN THE HOME

Singles: Take charge of what you believe about marriage. Prioritize truth and reason over emotion and experience when it comes to relationship formation. Lean on the church for support in the early years of dating, courtship, engagement, and marriage.

Spouses: Pursue your marriage with as much energy and excitement as you did your wedding. Submit to biblical authority for your marriage as you did your wedding. Take charge by plugging into a biblical community long after the rice is thrown.

Parents: Take charge of your family's discipleship in the home. Be intentional with the weeks and months you have left. Plug into biblical community and surround your children with additional voices of influence.

FAMILY CONVERSATION STARTERS

1. Why is a good name better than fine perfume?

2. Why is the day of death better than the day of birth?

3. What are some ways we look to the church during times of life change?

4. Think about the last time you attended a funeral. What questions did you ask? Did you make any life changing decisions? If so, what were they?

5. At the end of your life, what would you like to be known for?

CHAPTER 10

STARTING OVER

BREATHING LIFE INTO DEAD FAMILIES

"I want my every inhale infused with God's presence, my every exhale an extension of His presence."

—MARGARET FEINBERG

My friend Margaret Feinberg wrote a book called *The Sacred Echo,* which explains the way God works His Word into everyday life. For example, you read a passage of Scripture for your morning devotions and later that morning a friend shares that he read the same passage yesterday. You then discuss the text over coffee. Later that day, you visit your parents' house and notice the same passage on the verse-of-the-day calendar on their coffee table. That is the sacred echo.

We had a sacred-echo week recently. We were in Washington DC visiting National Community Church. As our family sat with friends in the back of the theater, the worship leader led us in a song about God breathing life into dead bones. I wept and placed my arm around my wife. Being in ministry often keeps families from worshipping together. Sad to say, moments like this are rare. I prayed and asked the Lord to restore my soul and breathe life into me and my family. Ministry can drain the life out of your marriage and family.

When we returned home to Branson, Amy and I reached for our Bibles and read together Ezekiel 37:

> The hand of the LORD was on me, and he brought me out by the Spirit of the LORD and set me in the middle of a valley; it was full of bones. He led me back and forth among them, and I saw a great many bones on the floor of the valley, bones that were very dry. He asked me, "Son of man, can these bones live?"
>
> I said, "Sovereign LORD, you alone know." Then he said to me, "Prophesy to these bones and say to them, 'Dry bones, hear the word of the LORD! This is what the Sovereign LORD says to these bones: I will make breath enter you, and you will come to life. I will attach tendons to you and make flesh come upon you and cover you with skin; I will put breath in you, and you will come to life. Then you will know that I am the LORD.'" So I prophesied as I was commanded. And as I was prophesying, there was a noise, a rattling sound, and the bones came together, bone to bone. I looked, and tendons and flesh appeared on them and skin covered them, but there was no breath in them. Then he said to me, "Prophesy to the breath; prophesy, son of man, and say to it, 'This is what the Sovereign LORD

says: Come, breath, from the four winds and breathe into these slain, that they may live.'" So I prophesied as he commanded me, and breath entered them; they came to life and stood up on their feet—a vast army. Then he said to me: "Son of man, these bones are the people of Israel. They say, 'Our bones are dried up and our hope is gone; we are cut off.' Therefore prophesy and say to them: 'This is what the Sovereign LORD says: My people, I am going to open your graves and bring you up from them; I will bring you back to the land of Israel. Then you, my people, will know that I am the LORD, when I open your graves and bring you up from them. I will put my Spirit in you and you will live, and I will settle you in your own land. Then you will know that I the LORD have spoken, and I have done it, declares the LORD.'" (verses 1–14)

God refreshes fatigued and tired believers. However, that's not what this text teaches. He breathes life into dead, decayed, and dried up bones. Is your marriage or family in the grave? Are you dead spiritually? Jesus still breathes life into dead people, marriages, and families. Thank you, Jesus!

A few days after God inspired us through Ezekiel 37, we met with close friends. Their marriage was dead. They were in the strategy stage of meeting with attorneys, planning custody, and dividing assets. For weeks we prayed and asked the Lord

Jesus still breathes life into dead people, marriages, and families.

to do a miracle in their home. Our prayer that week was simply, "Lord, breathe life into their marriage and family." It was all we knew to pray.

As we met over coffee that afternoon, the wife asked me, "Where's that Scripture in the Old Testament about the Valley of Dry Bones?"

I looked right at Amy with eyes that screamed, *"No way!"* It was a sacred echo. I love how God works. We sat there that day and watched God do a miracle. Both spouses had open hearts to God and to each other. They called off the divorce and committed to getting the help they needed. Amy and I went to bed that night rejoicing.

Are you open to a miracle in your marriage and family? Do you believe God still performs miracles today? I do. I saw one that Saturday afternoon. It doesn't mean the road to recovery will be easy. There will be moments of panic, fear, and anger. That's to be expected. The same power that saved our friends' marriage will sustain their marriage. They must stay fully charged with Jesus as their true and only Source of Life.

Our friends at the Focus on the Family National Institute of Marriage have worked with thousands of dead marriages over the past fourteen years. When God breathes life into a spouse or couple, the entire team rejoices. The team at NIM have full-time jobs watching God perform miracles.[23]

You must answer one question before you are officially registered for a marriage intensive at NIM: "Are you open to a miracle?" If both spouses answer that question with yes, they are invited to come. The team at NIM want to be a part of a miracle in that home. These miracles are possible because Jesus was raised from the dead!

The resurrection changed everything for you, your marriage, family, and future. According to 1 Corinthians 15:12–19, without the resurrection our preaching is useless, your faith is useless, we are false witnesses, and the grave is the end:

> But if it is preached that Christ has been raised from the dead, how can some of you say that there is no resurrection of the dead? If there is no resurrection of the dead, then not even Christ has been raised. And if Christ has not been raised, our preaching is useless and so is your faith. More than that, we are then found to be false witnesses about God, for we have testified about God that he raised Christ from the dead. But he did not raise him if in fact the dead are not raised. For if the dead are not raised, then Christ has not been raised either. And if Christ has not been raised, your faith is futile; you are still in your sins. Then those also who have fallen asleep in Christ are lost. If only for this life we have hope in Christ, we are of all people most to be pitied.

I recently spoke with a father who lost his son the week before Easter. I told him the day before Easter and three days before his son's funeral, "You know, tomorrow of all days is a great day to talk about the resurrection of the dead because the grave is not the end. We are no longer captives, but without the resurrection, you are still in bondage to sin. Without the resurrection, we are pitied for wasting our time."

Graveside at a funeral, we declare Jesus over the grave. Jesus has done everything necessary. He conquered the grave. He breathes life into dead people, marriages and families:

"Death has been swallowed up in victory."
"Where, O death, is your victory? Where, O death, is your sting?"
The sting of death is sin, and the power of sin is the law. But thanks be to God! He gives us the victory through our Lord Jesus Christ. (1 Corinthians 15:54–57)

Because of the resurrection, we are forgiven and rescued! Sometimes we focus on the forgiven part to the exclusion of the rescued part. Jesus rescues, heals, and restores. I want that for your marriage and family.

I watch way too many movies. My favorite scenes include the military commandos breaking down doors to rescue those in bondage. I can't fully explain it, but there are times I walk out at the end of the movie hoping something goes down so I can rescue someone. There's nothing in my history that supports my ability to do so, but my heart is racing nonetheless. Everyone loves a rescue story.

Because of the resurrection, we are forgiven and rescued!

When we walk down the street, I'm in constant protection mode over my family. I'm alert to our surroundings so that in case something happens, I can throw my family to safety while I take the hit. When I sit in a restaurant with Amy,

I want the vantage point. I want to see the door in case something goes down. I want to be her hero. I rehearse the maneuvers in my head.

The gospel of Jesus Christ is the greatest rescue of all time. We are in bondage to sin and Jesus breaks down the door and rescues us. That deserves a shout of praise! No movie will ever compete with that story. It is the greatest story ever told!

Will you allow Jesus to break down the door of your home and rescue you? Will you cry out for that rescue? Will you pray for that rescue for family members who are far from God?

Let's pray.

Heavenly Father,

We come to You thanking You for Your design for the family. You created us, and You sustain us. We would not be here right now if it weren't for You.

Guard our homes from the attacks of the world. We want our homes to honor, enjoy and prioritize marriage. We seek to honor our commitments to each other. We will treat each other as personally autographed by You.

Thank You for our homes and the ability to work to provide for them. We want to earn, give, and save as wise stewards. We receive with thanksgiving all we have from You. We are stewards, not owners. Thank You for our clothes, food, and shelter. We are grateful.

We thank You for salvation. We repent of our sins and turn to You. You are the Lord of our homes, and we choose to love You with all of our hearts, souls, minds, and strength. We want to love others with the same love and power You show us. You are the true and only Source of Life.

We ask that You comfort and heal the marriages and families around us that are struggling and calling it quits. Use our family to encourage other families. We choose to speak life over them. We want to bless them.

Cover us. Protect us. Use us to bring glory to You.

In Jesus' mighty name we pray, Amen.

EMPOWERING EVERYONE IN THE HOME

Singles: Jesus breathes life into dead people. Never lose hope in life because Jesus is the hope of the world. He is your hope and salvation.

Spouses: Jesus breathes life into dead marriages. Pray for the resurrection of dead marriages around you. The same power that raised Jesus from the dead is the same power that resurrects dead relationships.

Parents: Jesus breathes life into dead families. Never give up on your children. If they are far from God, pray and believe God for a miracle. Jesus rescues and restores, and He can restore your broken relationship with an adult child.

FAMILY CONVERSATION STARTERS

1. What can we do to speak life to each other?
2. What is the greatest rescue story you have ever heard?
3. How does Jesus breathe life into us?
4. Who do we need to pray for today?
5. Let's pray for our home and the families all around us.

ENDNOTES

1 http://www.familylife.com/about-us/what-we-believe/the-family-manifesto#.VFKFrc3Doxo

2 Quoted from Focus on the Family's *The Family Project.*

3 These seven parenting motives are discussed in greater detail in my book, *Trophy Child: Saving Parents from Performance, Preparing Children for Something Greater Than Themselves* (Colorado Springs; David C. Cook, 2012).

4 http://www.washingtonpost.com/opinions/robert-samuelson-the-family-deficit/2014/10/26/966f78a8-5b97-11e4-bd61-346aee66ba29_story.html, estimates the Pew Research center.

5 http://www.nytimes.com/2013/09/22/fashion/weddings/divorce-after-50-grows-more-common.html?_r=0

6 www.youtube.com/watch?v=MqtG-XfxMC4

7 All of these lists are used with permission of the person who wrote each list.

8 H. Norman Wright, *Always Daddy's Girl: Understanding Your Father's Impact On Who You Are* (Ventura, CA; Regal Books, 2001), 193–195.

9 These three honor lists for Dad are used by permission of the people who wrote the lists.

10 Used with permission of Charles Billingsly.

11 http://www.christianity.com/devotionals/upwords-max-lucado/open-your-door-open-your-heart-upwords-week-of-october-8-14-11639250.html

12 This skills list is adapted from the S.H.A.P.E. assessment for Woodland Hills Family Church.

13 http://michaelhyatt.com/retirement.html

14 http://www.huffingtonpost.com/2012/12/02/income-happiness_n_2220693.html

15 http://www.psychologytoday.com/articles/200411/the-truth-about-compatibility

16 Ibid.

17 Ibid.

18 http://www.goodreads.com/quotes/555465-the-reason-that-marriage-is-so-painful-and-yet-wonderful

19 http://thegospelcoalition.org/article/four-things-god-says-singles, SEP 02, 2014 by Vaughan Roberts

20 Ibid.

21 http://www.answers.com/Q/What_does_the_music_term_harmony_mean

22 usmilitary.about.com.

23 For more information on the marriage intensive program, visit www.nationalmarriage.com.

ABOUT THE AUTHOR

Ted Cunningham is the founding pastor of Woodland Hills Family Church in Branson, Missouri, where he has ministered for the past thirteen years. He is the author of *Fun Loving You* and *Trophy Child* and the co-author of four books with Dr. Gary Smalley. He is a graduate of Liberty University and Dallas Theological Seminary.

Married to his wife, Amy, for nineteen years, they have two children, Corynn and Carson. They currently reside in Branson, Missouri.

FOR MORE INFORMATION

For more information about this and other valuable
resources visit www.salubrisresources.com.